Two Worlds of Islam

Two Worlds of

Islam

Interaction between

Southeast Asia and

the Middle East

Fred R. von der Mehden

University Press of Florida

Gainesville/Tallahassee/Tampa

Boca Raton/Pensacola/Orlando

Miami/Jacksonville

Copyright 1993 by the Board of Regents of the State of Florida
Printed in the United States of America on acid-free paper
All rights reserved
Book design by Louise OFarrell

Library of Congress Cataloging-in-Publication Data

Von der Mehden, Fred R.
Two worlds of Islam: interaction between Southeast Asia and the
Middle East / Fred R. von der Mehden.
p.   cm.
Includes bibliographical references (p.   ) and index.
ISBN 0-8130-1208-2 (alk. paper).—ISBN 0-8130-1209-0 (pbk.: alk.
paper)
1. Asia, Southeastern—Relations—Middle East.   2. Middle
East—Relations—Asia, Southeastern.   3. Muslims—Asia,
Southeastern—Politics and government.   I. Title.
DS525.9.M628V66   1993
959'.0097671—dc20   92-44707

The University Press of Florida is the scholarly publishing agency
for the State University System of Florida, comprised of Florida
A & M University, Florida Atlantic University, Florida International
University, Florida State University, University of Central Florida,
University of Florida, University of North Florida, University of
South Florida, and University of West Florida.

University Press of Florida
15 Northwest 15th Street
Gainesville, FL 32611

For Ashley Paige Davis

Contents

Tables

ix

Preface

 The Muslim world has traditionally held the belief that the Middle East is the center of the culture, history, and theology of Islam and that the periphery is composed of populations less fortunate in those attributes. Other Muslim peoples have usually been perceived as less knowledgeable about Islam and more tainted with non-Islamic ideas. Since the great majority of Muslims are non-Arab and modern communications have allowed more extensive interaction within the *ummah* (the community of Muslims), this perception needs rethinking. For example, Indonesia, the country with the world's largest Muslim population, has long been viewed as somehow less Muslim than its Arab counterparts, has been little studied by Middle Eastern scholars, and is considered outside the political and economic interests of the "center" of Muslim civilization.

This study is an analysis of the changing patterns of interaction between the Muslim worlds of the Middle East and Southeast Asia. The material is primarily focused on the post–World War II era, although the initial chapter also includes a summary of the earlier history of the subject. It is primarily concerned with those nations of the Middle East that have been most important in this interaction during the postwar decades: Egypt, Saudi Arabia, Libya, Turkey, Syria, Iraq, Iran, the Persian Gulf states, and Pakistan; other Middle Eastern nations have been peripherally involved in particular issues.

Southeast Asia includes two types of Muslim societies. There are those in states where the majority of the population is Muslim, primarily the large states of Malaysia and Indonesia but also the small, oil-rich sultanate of Brunei. Indonesia, with over 180 million people, is approximately 90 percent Muslim, while 52 percent of Malaysia's 17 million people are Muslim. There are also societies in states where the Muslim communities are minorities, principally the Philippines, Thailand, and Burma. None of these minority Muslim groups comprises more than 5 percent of the total population of their respective countries, and they tend to live in isolated areas. Southeast Asia's Muslims are almost entirely Sunni, although there is a small new Shi'i element in southern Thailand and some intellectual interest in Shi'i thought in cities such as Bangkok and Jakarta.

In this study three major areas of analysis—economic, political, and intellectual—are covered. Concerning the economy, the development of trade and investment between the Middle East and Southeast Asia is analyzed. The major proposition to be tested is whether there is a relationship between the common Islamic religious background of the two regions and aid, investment, and trade. In other words, was there any validity in Southeast Asian Muslim leaders' expectation that there was an economic advantage in being coreligionists with their wealthy Middle Eastern brethren?

Political issues considered here include the extent of Middle Eastern involvement in the domestic politics of Southeast Asia, through aid to Muslim minorities and alleged support of dissident groups in Indonesia and Malaysia, and the extent of Southeast Asian interest in Middle Eastern issues such as Israel's policy toward the Palestinians and its Arab neighbors, the Soviet invasion of Afghanistan, and inter-Arab conflicts. An important concern will be the degree to which such policies have been motivated by or publicly attributed to a religious basis. The political section will also cover the development of international Islamic organizations and the extent to which Southeast Asian Muslim groups and states have participated in them. A separate chapter will deal with the impact of Iran's Islamic Revolution on the political and religious life of Southeast Asians. The core of this chapter is from my essay in John Esposito, ed., *The Iranian Revolution.*

An analysis of the intellectual interaction that has developed between the two regions completes the book. It will cover the character of the penetration of Middle Eastern Islamic thinking into Southeast Asia, the means of transmitting new religious ideas, and changing patterns of interaction in recent decades.

The author wishes to thank the numerous individuals in Southeast Asia who showed great patience in answering questions regarding their religion and societies. Also deserving thanks are the librarians who provided much of the material necessary for writing this book, including the library staffs at the Institute of Southeast Asian Studies in Singapore, Ohio University, Northern Illinois University, Cornell University, and the University of California, Berkeley. Finally, Rice University provided the time and funds to allow me to concentrate on this effort.

Chapter 1

HISTORICAL BACKGROUND

 Southeast Asian Islamic historiography is replete with differing answers to the question of when the Arabs or Islam first arrived in Southeast Asia. There are equally varied adherents to the question of who initially transmitted the religion to the region, among proponents of the Arabs of Hadhramaut; the religious leaders and merchants from Bengal, Coromandel, and Gujarat in India; and even the Persians and Kurds.[1] This study is concentrated on the modern world of Islam and thus is only peripherally concerned with these discussions. Suffice it to state that Islam became an important force in parts of Southeast Asia in the fourteenth century and continued to expand thereafter.

THE EARLY ERA

There are three rather arbitrary periods of interaction between the Middle East and Southeast Asia: from the advent of Islam in the East to the early nineteenth century, from then to the end of World War II, and the postwar era. The bulk of this study is an analysis of the post–World War II period, but this chapter is concentrated on the first two periods. The events and processes discussed here have generally been covered in depth in the literature, and this review is simply intended to provide background information.

During the first several centuries after the coming of Islam to eastern Asia, there were intermittent formal and informal relations between the two regions. Trade continued but was increasingly sub-

1

jected to European economic, military, and political interference. Politically, the most significant Middle Eastern involvement was sixteenth-century Turkish aid to Southeast Asian opponents of their common enemy, the Portuguese. There developed a short-lived political and military alliance between Turkey and the Achenese sultanate, with military aid being sent by the Turks.[2] There continued to be a close relationship between the rulers of Constantinople and the Muslim population of the Indies until the twentieth century. There were also a number of cases in which Arabs or Turks advised local traditional rulers in the region, but this advice tended to be given on an individual rather than an international basis.

In terms of interaction between religion and intellectual life, Muslim thought began entering into Southeast Asia through religious personnel, primarily from the Middle East and India. Southeast Asians also now began taking the arduous *haj* (pilgrimage) to Mecca and Indonesian students of Islam, in particular, began studying at places like Cairo, Mecca, and Medina.[3]

For a period Southeast Asia was the recipient of Arab civilization, often filtered through India. The influence of Sufism was particularly important at this time. The more mystical and flexible aspects of Sufism were attractive to Southeast Asians and aided the adoption of Islam in the region. There was probably no question among Muslims in both regions as to which was superior in terms of knowledge and religious legitimacy. Nor was there any real expectation that Islam in Southeast Asia would or perhaps should be a major intellectual and political force in the Muslim world. As we shall see, this pattern also tended to permeate the next era.

NINETEENTH AND EARLY TWENTIETH CENTURIES

Economic Interaction

Economic interaction between the Middle East and Southeast Asia during the century prior to World War II was limited. The Middle East was economically weak in this period and had neither the wealth nor the industry to avail itself of raw materials from the East. For example, the *Malayan Yearbook* for 1939 named no Middle Eastern nation within its lists of import and export leaders.[4] The Dutch East Indies that year showed a similar pattern for export and import leaders, although there a small amount of fibers were imported and about 20 percent of the archipelago's tea went to the Middle East.[5] No doubt, the major economic interaction between the two regions related to expenditures by Southeast Asian pilgrims and students in Arabia and Egypt.

Political Interaction

Politically, most action centered upon Southeast Asian relations with the Ottoman Empire, the role of Pan-Islam, involvement in the questions that followed the fall of the caliphate after World War I, and fears among colonial administrators over possible undesirable religio-political effects of the pilgrimage and study in the Middle East. During the period under discussion, Dutch administrators, in particular, worried considerably that peace and order were endangered by unsettling influences from the haj and study in the Middle East.[6] Early in the nineteenth century the Dutch attempted to make the haj difficult by taxation and passport restrictions, and various debilitating regulations lasted through the century. However, the development of better transportation and growing stability in the Dutch East Indies led to considerable growth in the number of pilgrims. Their numbers increased from some two thousand a year at mid-century to between seven thousand and eleven thousand by the end of the century.

Colonial administrators feared possible religio-political "fanaticism" from returning pilgrims, noting that many local "agitators" had made the haj. For example, in Banten, the scene of government-religious conflict, the number of pilgrims increased from 59 in 1887 to 827 in 1896, leading the authorities to see "in every Muslim scholar (*kiyai*) an enemy." This developed into what was termed *hajiphobia* in the Dutch administration.[7] Although the vast majority of those returning remained apolitical in their actions, they must have been deeply affected by their experiences and must have developed a heightened feeling of religious identity. As W. Roff has noted, the effect of even brief exposure to a wholly Muslim environment, in which all authority was subject to the laws of God, was by no means negligible. In such an environment, the universality of the faith was demonstrated by a congregation of pilgrims of all races, from all levels of society. They were visibly joined in a leveling, and, at the same time, an exalting religious experience. Even sojourners could hardly fail to be impressed by the greatness of the Islamic peoples or escape sharing the common knowledge of the manner in which so much of Islam had become politically subordinate to the West and to Christianity.[8]

Part of this negative colonial reaction also arose because of questions about the effects of the symbolic power given Muslim leaders by the haj and the economic resources lost to the archipelago. The British tended to be less disturbed by the impact of the pilgrimage and made efforts to facilitate it, a policy not developed by the Dutch until the beginning of the twentieth century. Both established programs to improve pilgrims' health and living conditions and control undesirable elements who sought to exploit the pilgrims. This paternalistic colonial policy did not necessarily find favor from the pilgrims, who found British and Dutch authorities waiting to examine them upon their arrival in Arabia.

European administrators also worried about the increasing number of Arabs coming to the region, resulting in perhaps over twenty thousand residing in the Indies and Malaya toward the end of the nineteenth century. The Arabs tended to be given considerable respect by the local Muslim population because of the inclusion of an important minority of learned Muslim teachers in their ranks, their ability to speak Arabic, and the holy place from which they came. This respect produced fears of an expanded Arab economic and political role and more support for Pan-Islam in colonial Southeast Asia. Again, restrictions were formulated, this time on Arab residence and travel.

The twentieth century also saw a significant increase in the number of pilgrims and students going to the Middle East, a further worry for authorities, particularly during a period of increased pan-Islamic efforts. Malaya is said to have sent the largest number of pilgrims per capita from South-Southeast Asia, reaching a high of fourteen thousand in 1920.[9] The number of pilgrims from the Indies increased from 7,421 in 1900–1901 to a high of 123,052 in 1926–27.[10] This growth must be seen against the backdrop of the rise of what was perceived as a more doctrinally oriented regime in Arabia under the Wahabbis and Ibn Saud, who in his first years of power briefly toyed with efforts to foster pan-Islamic ideas. This added to the concern of the colonial authorities and led to reinstatement of some pilgrimage restrictions in the Indies.

There was also an increase in the number of individuals who remained in the Middle East for additional religious study. Some stayed in Mecca and Medina, others in Cairo. Exact numbers are difficult to ascertain, but D. van der Muelen, who served with the Dutch government in Arabia during World War II, reports that more than two thousand residents of Arabia claimed to be citizens of the Indies who received Dutch government aid.[11] In Cairo approximately eighty Southeast Asian students were studying in 1919 (three-fourths were Indonesian), but this number increased substantially after 1922 with the improvement of the economy in Malaya and the Indies. By 1925 there were about two hundred Southeast Asian students in Cairo.[12] Although the depression of the 1930s brought a decrease in both the haj and students studying abroad, there was still a significant student population in the late 1930s; in 1937–38 there were 10,884 pilgrims going to Mecca from the Indies.

While hajiphobia continued, there was also criticism of the type of political education obtained in Egypt. The sultan of Selangor, for example, worried about the kind of undesirable ideas that might be picked up by Malays from other pilgrims or students from Sumatra, Java, and elsewhere, and he disapproved of sending young men to Egypt.[13] This concern on the part of authorities in Malaya and Indonesia had a real foundation, for as one Malay commented, "In Mecca one could study religion only; in Cairo, politics as well."[14] Throughout this period the Middle East was a hotbed of nationalist fervor, and it would have been surprising if these young Southeast Asians had not been affected. They formed local associations, published a monthly magazine in Cairo, and articulated nationalist causes in their homelands. In 1945 Indonesians living in the Middle East were among the first people living overseas to support independence for their country.[15]

It must have also distressed the colonial administrations when Malay students and workers residing abroad showed their unity. The first Malay-Indonesian society, Jami'ah Al-Kairiah, formed in Cairo in 1922, established a monthly, *Seruan Aazhar*, the purpose of which was "to bring radiance and light to our (joint) homeland."[16] Elsewhere in the Middle East, students formed Persatuan Tababah Indonesia Malaya (PERTINDOM, or the Association of Indonesian and Malay Students) in Saudi Arabia, and in Iraq the Majlis Kebangsaan Indonesia-

Malaya (MAKINDOM, or the National Council of Indonesia-Malaya), later the Perkumpulan Permuda Indonesia (PPI, or the Convention of Indonesian Youth), which included Malays within its membership.

A second set of Middle East–Southeast Asian political issues that dominated the late nineteenth century and the twentieth century before 1945 centered on Turkey. The colonial powers were particularly embarrassed by the support Malay and Indonesian Muslims gave to the caliph, who many Southeast Asians viewed as their religious and even true temporal leader.

During the late nineteenth century considerable worry was expressed in Dutch political circles about possible Turkish involvement in domestic matters in the Indies.[17] The Dutch were identified in the texts and newspapers of the Middle East as oppressors of their Muslim charges. C. Snouck Hurgronje, a famous scholar on Islam, noted that "in the Muslim daily press our government is frequently derided as the enemy of Muslims, while in the geographical textbooks used in Turkish and Arab schools the Netherlands is tersely indicated as a Power unfamiliar with the principles of tolerance, under whose yoke millions of Muslims suffer."[18] Newspapers in Egypt, Constantinople, and Beirut had correspondents in the Indies and Singapore who regularly reported on the mistreatment of fellow Muslims. In the second half of the nineteenth century there were reports of efforts to obtain Turkish aid for the Achenese of north Sumatra who were attempting to ward off Dutch colonial control. This followed other charges of Turkish contacts with anti-Dutch forces in earlier part of the century. The Achenese made major efforts to get help from Constantinople and did receive considerable sympathy from powerful officials in the Ottoman capital. The Turks offered to mediate the conflict, and they even broached the idea of Constantinople's suzerainty over Acheh, but all came to naught as Acheh was incorporated into the Dutch East Indies.[19]

At the end of the century, an active Turkish consul in Batavia exacerbated Dutch fears by encouraging Indonesians to come to him for advice and to view themselves as subjects of the caliph. He also made contact with nobility who opposed Dutch rule; he was ultimately recalled at the request of colonial authorities.[20] Over the following decades, Indonesian political leaders tended to be far more supportive of Turkey than were their Malay counterparts. Even prior to World

War I Indonesians expressed sympathy for the Turkish positions in the Balkans and Tripoli. During the war, Dutch officials and newspapers in the Indies feared that local Indonesians would support Turkey, thus weakening Dutch neutrality. There were tales of pictures of the caliph in Indonesian homes and reports of submarines of Turkey's ally, Germany, aiding dissidents in the archipelago. Reality was more apparent when, for example, a 1915 nationalist organization in Solo, Java, asked Turkey for advice regarding the plague in the area. This request reflected a general pattern of Indonesians approaching the Turkish consulate for guidance.[21] Backed by the local indigenous press Indonesians gave generously to the Red Crescent, and the newspapers also supported the Turkish cause on such issues as the Armenian question.[22] All of these factors were distressing to the colonial governments, and in the Indies there is some reason to believe that local nationalists used some of these tactics for just that effect. However, they also showed that many Indonesians wanted to participate more fully in wider Muslim affairs.

The British faced a different situation in Malaya. Although the United Kingdom and Commonwealth countries were at war with the Turks and their allies, the Malay leadership was still primarily in the hands of the more traditional Malay aristocracy.[23] Before the war the British faced many of the same problems as did the Dutch, although usually on a smaller and less emotional scale than in the Indies. London's direct involvement in such conflicts, as those with the Mahdi in the Sudan and Egyptian revolts, gave local Muslims reasons to oppose these British policies against coreligionists. As in the Indies, there was sympathy for prewar Turkish problems with the Europeans, financial aid by local Muslims to the Red Crescent, and the expression of pan-Islamic sentiments.

The British also worried about the impact of the haj and Arab immigrants. Official attitudes were, perhaps, reflected in the call for the Arabs to be sent "back to Arabia, or [be ordered] to proceed to Arabia on pain of punishment [for] disobedience. If an example is made of one of these holy men, the others will be quiet in future. The Arabs are, however, fond of money and collect it under cover of their holy character. Fear for their worldly possessions will keep them quiet."[24]

During World War I there was less sympathy in Malaya for the Turks and their allies than in Indonesia. The British government ac-

tively carried out propaganda campaigns against their wartime enemies, and the Malay sultans supported the British and asked their
people not to aid Turkey. The sultans backed aid projects for the
British cause, called for public prayers for British success, and joined
with other leaders in celebrating the victorious end of the war. Commentators have observed that the situation in Malaya can be explained by Malaya's economic growth during the war, active British
efforts to control any undesirable religio-political issues, the fact that
Malay leadership came from a conservative aristocracy rather than the
more urban and often secular nationalists of the Indies, and a history
there of a more flexible colonial religious policy toward Muslims.[25]

In the 1920s Pan-Islam became a prominent issue in Southeast
Asian politics, particularly in Indonesia. Unlike the nineteenth century, when the movement in the region was dominated by Arabs and
Turks residing in Malaya and the Indies, this time it was primarily led
by indigenous nationalists. The two main issues concerned the future
of the caliphate and attitudes among Southeast Asians toward the
new Turkey under Kemal Attaturk. Although the caliphate as both a
symbol and a real power had been decreasing in legitimacy during the
nineteenth century, many throughout the Muslim world were reluc-
tant to see this symbol of unity end. A series of international conferences was held to try to formulate a common policy. After these
efforts proved abortive, the next focus was the new, more secular
government in Turkey.

Again, Malaya displayed far less interest than the Indies in the caliphate movement and international organizational activities among
Muslims. Delegations from Malaya were sent to two international
conferences dealing with the caliphate, but one delegation was described as being of low quality and the other was composed only of
Arabs from Singapore.[26] Nor was there heavy coverage in Malayan
newpapers or mass meetings in support of the caliphate, although
there was one report of a meeting of unknown size that voted 72
percent for its continuation.[27] The Kemalist revolution, on the other
hand, had mixed reviews. Many applauded economic and political
developments, but others of the aristocracy and religious communities were less pleased with the secular tone of the new regime.
However, the end of the caliphate inevitably led to a decline in interest in Turkey within British Malaya.

The caliphate issue was important within the Indonesian nationalist and religious communities for a relatively brief period in the twenties. Interest about it was based on a combination of historic pan-Islamic sentiments, a desire to participate in the wider Muslim community, and political exigencies. As previously noted, elements of the Islamic community had exhibited strong interest in Pan-Islam in the nineteenth century. During World War I, the Turkish government had attempted to develop Pan-Islam with funds from sources in British India.[28] Yet, a review of discussions and activities of the major Muslim nationalist organization, Sarekat Islam (SI), shows little apparent involvement with Pan-Islam from 1913 to 1919. By 1920 two factors came together to give emphasis to Pan-Islam within the nationalist movement. One was the victory of the secular Turkish revolution that raised the issue of the future of the caliphate. Given previous Indonesian support for the symbolic nature of the caliphate, there was considerable interest in religious circles regarding events in the Middle East. At the same time, the more religious leadership of Sarekat Islam was being challenged by the communists who were seeking to infiltrate the party.[29]

Local communists were faced with attempting to explain away well-publicized international communist attacks on Pan-Islam. They were particularly disturbed by the criticisms of Pan-Islam at the second Commintern congress and tried to argue that, properly understood, Pan-Islam could work alongside anti-imperialism. However, the communists recognized that, although the Muslim nationalists might be with them "with their stomachs," their hearts remained "with their heaven, which we cannot give them."[30] This dilemma was also apparent with regard to the caliphate question. Muslim nationalists endeavored to counter the communists by exploiting both Pan-Islam and the caliphate issue.[31] As I have written elsewhere: "Having lost large sections of its followers as a result of Dutch actions, poor administration, indiscretions of local S.I. [Sarekat Islam] groups, and flirtations with the secular left, the S.I. hoped to gain a double advantage from Pan-Islam by reuniting the Muslim groups behind its banner and counterbalancing the secular nationalists. Thus, its involvement with Pan-Islam coincided with the struggle against left-wing elements within the movement."[32]

To these ends, the more religious leaders in the nationalist movement attempted a variety of tactics. Starting in 1922, SI and the Muhammadiyah, the Modernist religio-educational association, organized ten annual Al-Islam conferences. The delegates discussed a wide range of matters arising out of events in the Middle East, including the caliphate question, the future of Palestine, and the Greco-Turkish war. However, the major organ for promoting Pan-Islam became the East Indies branch of the Islamic World Congress (Moe'tamaroel Alamil Islami, or MAIHS).

The caliphate question particularly intrigued a number of Modernist Islamic nationalist leaders in the Indies. Indonesian representatives, funded by local donations, were sent to the 1926 caliphate congress in Cairo where they were to propose a council of Muslim countries that would elect a president who would take the title of caliph. The conference was not particularly successful, in large part because another congress was called for Mecca for the following year (one SI representative, its president, did not even go to Cairo, remaining in Arabia). With the failure of the Mecca meeting and obvious policy differences within the Muslim world, the caliphate movement went into a speedy decline and all but expired.

There were positive and negative results for the Indonesian Muslims who had participated in this activity relating to the caliphate. On the positive side, there was a short-term strengthening of both the position of the religious leadership in Sarekat Islam against their secular opponents and the bonds among Muslims in the Indies. It also gave some international prominence to Indonesian Muslims who, for the first time, were recognized as having a role to play in world Islamic affairs. The Egyptians, in particular, were pleased to see the Indonesians attend the Cairo meeting, thus reflecting broad international support for Egyptian efforts.

However, these efforts were ultimately negative in that they displayed the weaknesses of Islamic political organization. There was considerable difficulty in obtaining the small monetary amount needed to send delegates and, in fact, the 11,000 florins that were needed were not collected. The delegates chosen were not fluent in either Arabic or English, the languages of the meetings, and, in the words of one Middle Eastern observer, they were "a weak people in every matter."[33] These activities ultimately reinforced divisions within the Muslim community in the Indies, as SI and the Muhammadiyah competed for leadership. Further, more conservative Muslims op-

posed Pan-Islam. They were antagonized by both its Modernist Islamic leadership and the achievement of power in the holy cities of
Arabia by the Wahabbis, led by Ibn Saud.

Although Pan-Islam remained important in Indonesian Islamic circles and other organizations rose to foster its cause, the rest of the
prewar period found it at the periphery of subjects discussed among
local nationalists. Still, there were reports in the 1930s of Dutch fears
that Ibn Saud had really not given up on Pan-Islam,[34] and during
World War II there were negative reactions within the Indonesian
community to the treatment of the Grand Mufti, who some saw as a
claimant to the caliphate.[35]

Thus, with regard to political matters, the colonial authorities in
Southeast Asia, particularly those in the Indies, saw the relationship
between the Muslims in the Middle East and those in their colonies in
negative terms. Many Europeans believed that the haj increased religious "fanaticism" and encouraged loyalties outside the colony. The
returning pilgrims were suspected of undermining peace and order.
Both the pilgrims and the students studying in the Middle East were
viewed as recipients of undesirable political and religious ideas from
Arabians, Egyptians and from Asians from India and other colonies.

The authorities were probably quite correct in their presumptions
concerning many of the students who lived in the nationalistic environment of interwar Cairo. However, as can be seen from the publications of religious leaders trained in the Middle East, many students
came back to Southeast Asia with conservative religious and largely
apolitical views. No doubt, many pilgrims returned with a new sense
of religious identity and dissatisfaction at being ruled by a Christian
government.

However, the hajiphobia that was particularly prevalent among
Dutch administrative and commercial interests in the Indies did not
reflect reality. A large number of pilgrims were elderly individuals or
civil servants fulfilling one of the core requisites of Islam. As can be
seen from the variations between prewar Malaya and Indonesia, governmental policies responded to the political and religious dangers of
the pilgrimage differently. Still, for those residing in these colonies,
the haj gave hundreds of thousands of Muslims the opportunity to
escape colonial rule for a brief period and to participate in a religiously inspiring act that reinforced the universality and vitality of
their faith. To colonial rulers this was, at the least, unsettling.

Nor could colonial authorities view the long-term relationship between Muslims in Southeast Asia and those ruling in Constantinople
in positive terms. While little came out of efforts to involve the Ottoman Empire in Southeast Asian affairs and the caliphate movement
proved abortive, the identification with the rulers of Turkey was de-
cried by the authorities. Beliefs that the caliph was the spiritual and,
to some, the ultimate temporal leader of the Islamic world weakened
the authority and legitimacy of colonial rule. Sympathy for the Turkish cause in the first two decades of the twentieth century threatened
Dutch neutrality and caused problems for the British, who were at
war with Turkey. The caliphate movement underscored questions of
the legitimacy of colonial authority, increased political awareness
among local Muslims, and brought those Muslims into contact with
the international Islamic community.

The first three decades of the twentieth century were years of considerable religion-based political activity in Southeast Asia and in the
Indies in particular. In that volatile atmosphere, Pan-Islam was considered to have the potential of undermining colonial authority and
bringing Southeast Asian Muslims in contact with "undesirable" elements outside Southeast Asia. Again, it came to little and the British
were less worried about the movement than the Dutch. There were
even periods when Pan-Islam may have been looked at more benignly
by the latter, as when SI leaders used it against the communists. In
fact, from a historical perspective, the various formal efforts to advance Pan-Islam ultimately had relatively little long-term impact on
Southeast Asia. This does not mean that the identification of local
Muslims with the wider Islamic community and their sympathy for
treatment of fellow Muslims by other colonial regimes did not influence political and religious thinking in the region. It is, however,
necessary to delineate between the more institutionalized attempts to
foster Pan-Islam and popular support for the unity of the ummah.
This brings us to the third aspect of the relationship between the
Middle East and Southeast Asia.

Intellectual Influences

The intellectual currents to be covered in this section have been analyzed in depth elsewhere and will only be discussed briefly here.[36]

Throughout the nineteenth and early twentieth centuries both traditional and new religious ideas flowed into Islamic Southeast Asia
from abroad. The transmission came through learned local *ulama* (Islamic scholars) trained in the Middle East, Arab and South Asian
scholars who came to Southeast Asia, and books and pamphlets published in both areas.[37] Of particular importance were the Jawa, as
Southeast Asians staying in Mecca were termed. These included well-
respected religious scholars who passed on their learning both in the
Holy City and upon their temporary or permanent return to Southeast Asia. Within Southeast Asia itself, Singapore was an important
center for the dissemination of Islamic ideas. A major pilgrimage port
and home for foreign Muslim scholars, it offered a base for those who
could not go to Mecca for study.[38] Within the region, Singapore,
Penang, and the Indies transmitted the new ideas of the Middle East
into other Muslim communities in the Malay areas of Malaya and the
Philippines, but the latter areas did not function in that role for the
Middle East.

Beyond the transmission of traditional legal and theological scholarship, two major streams of Islamic thought that were particularly
important in this period were Sufism and Modernism.[39] The introduction of Sufi thought goes back to the advent of Islam into the region. It
was brought to the Indies by Muslim scholars from the Middle East and
India and by returning students even before the nineteenth century.[40]
In the years that followed, Sufi orders in the Middle East, such as the
Qadiryya and Naqshbandiyya, attracted many pilgrims who in turn
went home to disseminate Sufi thought and establish local branches of
the orders.

However, during the century before World War II, the intellectual
import from the Middle East with the greatest impact on public Islam
in Southeast Asia was the Modernist movement. Coming out of Egypt
at the end of the nineteenth century, Modernist thought demanded a
purification of the faith. Modernist reformers rejected the overlay of
traditional interpretations and philosophies of medieval Islam as well
as the "non-Islamic" elements that had accrued to the religion in
Malaya and the Indies. The syncretic, often pre-Islamic practices of
the region were criticized, and the individual was called upon to be
his own interpreter of the scriptures. The Modernists, often called
Kuam Muda or New Group (as against the Kuam Tua or Old Group or

Faction), supported *itjihad*, the independent interpretation of Islamic law. They encouraged the learning of Arabic to allow the believer to do that analysis. Politically, they became arrayed against more conservative religious groups and local religious authorities who saw them as a challenge to their legitimacy.

Modernism was particularly potent in the Indies at both regional and national levels. The Kuam Muda movement was also an important intellectual, political, and educational force in Malaya between the world wars. In Malaya reformist activity was especially prevalent in Singapore, Penang, and Perak. For example, in Perak the noted reformist school Maahad Il-Ehya Assyarif Gunung Semanggul (MIAGUS) was established in the 1930s and was quickly strengthened by graduates and teachers from Egypt and Saudi Arabia.[41] Out of that school came many postwar activists.

In the Indies the Modernist movement gained considerable momentum in the first three decades of the twentieth century, with an obvious debt owed to its Middle Eastern connection. In Batavia (Jakarta), it initially developed within the Arab community. A Modernist school was established, and one of its key mentors was a Sudanese. Minangkabau, in west Sumatra, was an early center for Modernist thinking, even supplying support to MIAGUS and writers of the first Modernist newspaper in the region, *Al-Iman*, inaugurated in Singapore in 1906. The imam of the Shafi'i school of law at the Masjid al-Haram in Mecca, Ahmad Khatib, was the teacher to many Minangkabaua scholars. He, too, was from Minangkabau.[42] Many Indonesians from Sumatra and Java were also trained in Egypt. They brought back the Modernist ideas that spread throughout Cairo and later imported Egyptian texts to be used in the schools they founded upon their return to Southeast Asia.

The most important Modernist organization, the Muhammadiyah, was formed in 1911 in Jogjakarta. It ultimately grew into what James Peacock has called "certainly the most powerful Islamic movement ever to exist in Southeast Asia."[43] The Muhammadiyah became heavily involved in education, clinics, and social change.[44] Its founder, Ahmad Dahlan, as well as many others in its core leadership, studied under Ahmad Khatib in Mecca, and others were trained in Cairo by the followers of the great Modernist Mohammed Abduh. However, the very size and number of schools of the organization meant varied interpretations of its mission and of Modernism itself. Thus, in Minangkabau, there was a greater emphasis on purifying the faith, and the activists reflected greater Middle Eastern intellectual influence. On Java, the priority was more in competing with Western challenges and Modernism appeared to reflect local issues.

In reviewing the intellectual relationship between Muslims in the two regions, it is obvious that, as with the previously discussed political issues, the Middle East was the primary source of religious thought for Southeast Asia. Many of the new ideas that arose in Muslim centers such as Cairo and Mecca in the century before World War II found fertile ground in the East, but the seminal writing remained in the Middle East. There were learned and respected individual religious scholars from Malaya and the Indies residing in places such as Mecca. In fact, as in the development of Modernism, these places could act as transmitters between scholars in the two regions. However, there was no cohesive body of thought arising from Southeast Asia that significantly influenced religious developments in the Middle East or South Asia. Often the most interesting intellectual analyses that developed in Southeast Asia were, indeed, the reinterpretation of ideas imported into the region to fit the needs of the new political and social environments in which they came to rest.

THE TRANSITION

The remainder of this study will concentrate upon the postwar, post-independence era. However, it is important to note how the changed conditions that came with independence significantly affected the environment in which interaction between the Muslim worlds of the Middle East and Southeast Asia operated. This transition had four major elements. First, the attainment of independence by states in both regions broke the official barriers between these countries that had been maintained by the colonial powers. This change allowed the implementation of formal diplomatic relations and participation in international Islamic organizations at an official level. It also facilitated trade and investment opportunities. However, as we shall see, it did not necessarily quiet fears of state authorities regarding possible dangers to domestic order arising out of religiopolitical contacts with the Middle East.

Underscoring these worries has been the increased interest shown by governments in both regions to promote themselves to Muslim peoples abroad in the name of Islam. Thus, for example, the Saudis have competed with the Libyans and Iranians for the minds of Southeast Asian Muslims through public and allegedly clandestine means. On their part, the Malaysians have actively participated in worldwide Islamic organizations and spoken on political issues facing Muslims in the Middle East for both domestic and foreign policy reasons. Both they and the Indonesians have attempted to play upon their religious ties with the Middle East to develop trade, loans, and investment opportunities.

A third change has been the development of more sophisticated means of transmitting ideas, allowing Muslims to more easily reach one another across the Islamic world. Aiding this development has been the great increase in the number of publications and translations dealing with Muslim subjects. Contemporary Middle Eastern writers now have their books regularly published and translated in Southeast Asia, and Muslim periodicals provide their readers with translations of these works. The dissemination of this literature is greatly facilitated by the major increase in literacy in both regions. Literacy in the prewar Indies was only approximately 7 percent for the indigenous population. By the mid-1980s, adult literacy was above 25 percent and almost all the youth of primary school age were attending school.[45] At the university level, there has been a major increase in the number of Southeast Asians studying Islamic subjects in both the Middle East and at Western institutions in Europe, Canada, and the United States.

Finally, there is increasing wealth in both regions. Obviously oil has brought major changes for many Middle Eastern states. Funds have become available for many governments in the Middle East, such as Saudi Arabia, to disseminate Islamic values. In addition, increased income, combined with education, has allowed the purchase of publications originating abroad. In Southeast Asia, Indonesia now has a middle-income economy, as has Thailand, which experienced the best continuous economic growth of any Asian country in the 1980s. Malaysia is moving into the upper-middle-income category.

All of these factors have promoted an expansion of political, economic, and intellectual ties within the ummah, creating the significantly different environment of the postwar era to which we now turn.

Chapter 2

ECONOMIC INTERACTION

 The 1970s and 1980s have seen a major increase in economic activity between the Middle East and Southeast Asia. This chapter will be devoted to trade, aid, and investment involving Muslim countries in the two regions during the postwar period. In the process an attempt will be made to answer two questions: What has been the level of direct support to Muslims in Southeast Asia for religious purposes? Also, was there any credence to Southeast Asian Muslim leaders' initial expectation that their countries would be preferred recipients of financial dealings with Middle Eastern states because of a mutuality of religious belief? In this sort of analysis, issues of timing may be crucial. Most particularly, does aid with religious connotations appear to correlate with particular policy goals of Middle Eastern states? For example, was there a major increase in Saudi activity following the Iranian Revolution due to the possible need to counter Iranian political-religious influence? Or did increased trade, aid, and investment more obviously parallel the greater availability of petrodollars following the 1973 oil crisis?

RELIGIOUS SUPPORT

The most obvious economic aid with religious ties has been the large number of instances in which funds have been given to mosques, Islamic political and educational organizations, missionary activities, and other Islamically oriented institutions. Since the mid-1950s there have been regular references to gifts from Middle Eastern govern-

17

ments or government-subsidized institutions to Southeast Asian religious organizations. Thus, King Faud of Saudi Arabia was one of the earliest sponsors of the Muslim College in Petaling Jaya, Malaysia. In 1964 a foundation stone was laid at the college to build a hall in Faud's name in honor of his previous eleven years of support, and the Saudis gave M$200,000 for the hall and M$15,000 for the yearly upkeep.[1] The previous year, at the urging of the president of the World Muslim League in Singapore, King Faisal of Saudi Arabia agreed to give S$128,250 for a Muslim lecture hall in that city.[2] Later in the decade the Saudis donated funds to a mosque in Sarawak and supplied other gifts. During this same period they also provided a subsidy of £1,200 a year to the Muslim Association of the Philippines.

Two Malaysian institutions have received special attention from the Saudis, PERKIM, one of the country's major missionary organizations, and the International Islamic University (IIU). In the mid-seventies, the Saudis donated M$232,209 to PERKIM. In 1981 it was announced that US$781,908 had been given, including $593,109 to the Regional Islamic Dakwah Council for Southeast Asia and the Pacific or RISEAP ($297,619 from Rabitat al alam al Islami and $295,490 from the Saudi government), $178,809 for PERKIM's refugee division, and $10,000 from two Saudi philanthropists.[3] The Saudis have aided the IIU from the beginning, too, although not to the extent originally hoped by the Malaysians.

Saudi support also was provided via a variety of nonofficial entities in Indonesia before a 1978 law authorized that all such external financial aid was to be channeled through the Jakarta government. Thus, in August 1978 the Saudis gave approximately $8 million (R340,000,000) to organizations such as the Nahdatul Ulama, Muhammadiyah, the Kiblat Center, and various Islamic schools.[4]

Other countries gave direct religious support as well, although usually not as much as the Saudis. In 1978, Kuwait's mufti visited Malaysia and, on behalf of his government, gave M$15,000 to the Perak State Religious Affairs Department for missionary work among the Orang Asli (indigenous jungle people). The mufti expressed his hope that "more Orang Asli will embrace the Islamic faith with more teachers being sent out to the jungles to educate them on the teachings of Islam."[5] Malaysia was one of seven countries, and the only Southeast Asian state, that received support for mosque building from

Iraq in 1980. The gulf emirates have been benefactors to PERKIM, and the IIU has received a wide range of gifts from Oriental rugs to support for faculty. Many Middle Eastern states have provided scholarships to Southeast Asian students for study in their countries, although the academic degrees supported were not all religious in content. (This aspect of Islamic education will be discussed further in chapter 4.)

Aside from Saudi Arabia, the most generous aid has come from Libya. It has also supported the IIU, helping to finance construction of science labs and the library, and has donated to organizations such as RISEAP. However, Libya has been most active as a benefactor for PERKIM. In the late 1970s, when former Malaysian prime minister Tengku Abdul Rahman was seeking funds for a new PERKIM head-quarters building, Libya provided a multimillion-dollar loan as well as over US$1 million for its operating budget. The following year, when the cost of the building rose, another major loan was obtained from Libya. Tengku saw only a religious rationale for this generosity, de-claring that "the main idea of Libya giving us this help is their desire to cooperate with us in all matters related to Islam."[6] This was cer-tainly the reason given by the Libyan government. As one Libyan official said when agreeing to provide assistance to the IIU, "The Libyan Government will not hesitate to offer assistance—technical and financial—to Malaysia in the spirit of Muslim brotherhood."[7]

Support for religious projects was not all one way. The Malaysians, in particular, have returned the favor. For example, in 1978 Malaysia agreed to donate M$562,000 worth of timber for building a mosque and religious center in Abasiya near Cairo.[8] There have been nu-merous examples of private funds raised to aid the Palestinian cause. These range from as little as M$300 in 1968 "from the Malaysian people" to M$170,000 in 1982 for the Palestine Liberation Organiza-tion from the Malaysian Dakwah organization, Angkatan Belia Islam Malaysia (ABIM).

It is difficult to determine if there were more than "purely reli-gious" factors involved in religious giving from major Middle Eastern donors such as Saudi Arabia and Libya. It would be overly cynical to see purely self-seeking motives in actions that appear to reflect a sincere wish to strengthen the Muslim faith in different regions of the world. It is also obvious that this was not simply a reaction to the Iranian Revolution as there were plentiful and generous donations from both countries before the Revolution. Further, many of the gifts were provided before the increased availability of petrodollars after the 1973 oil crisis.

It is also true that donors have sought to project an image of themselves as leaders in the Islamic world. Saudi Arabia, as the keeper of the holy places, has long considered itself to be the natural center of the Islamic world. Both before and after the Iranian Revolution it sought to underscore that position through religious donations. The Libyan government has also made an effort to obtain legitimacy among Muslims in Southeast Asia through gifts and involvement in the protection of Muslim interests in the region. Neither had to face a financial challenge of major proportions from the Iranians after Khoumeini's rise to power. Since the Revolution was followed by the Iran-Iraq War, which drained resources that might have been used for overseas proselytizing, the Iranian influence has been primarily seen as related to propaganda and clandestine operations (see chapter 3).

HAJ FINANCES

Perhaps one of the best examples of mutual financial benefits from religious activities has related to the haj. In earlier years the haj was largely financed by individual pilgrims, and the income accrued to private tour and transportation operators in Southeast Asia and Arabia. This system presented two problems to colonial and postindependence governments. Many haj operators were accused of gouging the pilgrims with inflated costs and poor accommodations. In addition, the older patterns meant that there was a considerable flow of capital out of Southeast Asia to those handling transportation to and tours in the Holy Land.

During the colonial period European administrators attempted to control the excesses related to the first problem and actively attempted to protect the pilgrims both at home and in Arabia. The independent governments of Southeast Asia sought to decrease the leakage of capital as well as continuing to enforce controls over possible infractions by tour operators.

The Indonesian government's actions are a good example of such policies.[9] The number of postwar pilgrims from Indonesia was significantly below prewar levels through the 1960s but increased markedly

Table 1. Indonesian Pilgrims, 1879–1982

Year	No. of pilgrims
1879–83	29,258
1884–88	17,115
1889–93	33,270
1894–98	41,575
1900–1902	19,192
1903–8	49,621
1909–13	122,354
1919–23	88,034
1924–28	138,842
1929–34	94,649
1935–40	37,212
1949–53	45,504
1954–58	62,963
1959–63	54,793
1964–69	77,680
1974–78	317,466
1979–82	240,241

Sources: Netherlands East Indies, *Indische Verslag,*
1931, 2:130, and Dhoffier, "Economic Effect," 57,
59, 66.

in the succeeding years.[10] (See table 1.) Variations of haj numbers
from throughout the region occurred because of internal and external
international issues, economic prosperity, and government policies.
Thus, in the immediate postwar decades both Indonesia and Malaysia faced severe insurgency problems related to the communist emer-
gency in Malaysia and rebellious activities in Indonesia. Indonesia
also suffered from difficult economic conditions during this period
and failed to sustain the economic levels attained prior to the war.

Economic hard times could, in turn, affect government policies
regarding the haj. Thus, periods of low agricultural prices in Malaysia
influenced government haj subsidies.[11] Bad economic conditions and
the resultant low levels of foreign exchange of postwar Indonesia led
that government to establish quotas on the number of pilgrims.[12]
These quotas were not abolished until 1969–70, when better eco-

Table 2. Cost of Haj Tickets (in US$) to and from Jakarta-Jeddah
and Total Garuda Earnings, 1974/75–1982/83

Year	No. of pilgrims	Cost of tickets	Total earnings
1974/75	53,752	715	38,432,680
1975/76	45,140	820	37,041,800
1976/77	17,904	840	15,039,360
1977/78	27,660	840	23,234,400
1978/79	73,030	840	61,345,200
1979/80	41,838	1,044	43,678,872
1980/81	75,998	1,306	99,253,388
1981/82	67,141	1,570	105,411,128
1982/83	55,264	1,652	91,296,128

Source: Dhoffier, "Economic Effects," 66.

nomic conditions and the thirty-five-day limit on time that pilgrims
could spend in Saudi Arabia decreased exchange burdens.

After 1969 the Indonesian government moved to a policy in which
it could further restrict foreign exchange losses, control the number
and treatment of pilgrims, and have its own financial monopoly over
pilgrim tours and transport. Specifically, private operators could no
longer organize pilgrims when that activity became an official monopoly. The government also moved to eliminate the exchange losses
previously experienced when international aircraft flew pilgrims to
Saudi Arabia. By restricting flights to the national airline, Garuda, it
could control haj numbers by lowering or raising flight costs. There is
ample evidence to show that these costs have caused fluctuations in
the annual size of the haj contingent.[13] The large number of pilgrims
carried by Garuda has been of great economic benefit to the government. (See table 2.) In addition, state banks have made great profits
from the exchange of foreign currency before and after pilgrims have
gone overseas.

Saudi Arabia has long found the haj a major means of foreign
exchange earnings from Southeast Asia. One study showed that in
1979–80 the total expenditure per Indonesian pilgrim in Saudi Arabia
was US$1,200 for living costs and services, approximately 45 percent

of the total haj cost to the pilgrim.[14] In 1981 this exchange brought to Saudi Arabia a total of US$76,663,605, divided as follows:[15] cost of renting Madinatul-Hujjaj, $1,670,468; Syekh service, $6,138,701; Naqabah, $6,160,186; accommodations, $28,190,491; direct pilgrim costs (mostly living expenses), $34,503,759. It is apparent that the haj is one of the most important components of economic interaction between Southeast Asia and the Middle East.

TRADE

As noted in chapter 1, prewar trade between Southeast Asia and the Middle East was a minor component of the total trade of either region. Nor was there large-scale economic activities for another twenty-five years after World War II. Foreign trade statistics for 1963 are presented in table 3 as an example.

Another major trading partner not noted in these data, Israel, was eliminated by the major Muslim states in the ensuing years. For political reasons Israeli trade was banned in Malaysia in 1974. In 1971 Malaysia had imported M$11.01 million of goods from Israel, mainly oranges and fertilizers, and had exported M$2.05 million in goods, primarily in rubber and tin.[16]

The first Malaysian trade mission had gone to the Middle East in 1969 in an effort to sell building materials, vegetable oils, and timber and to buy petroleum.[17] Initially, little trade developed. However, by 1973 major economic changes had taken place in Southeast Asia and the Middle East that would alter the character of economic relations between them. Growth rates of the oil-producing states of West Asia were remarkable, ranging from 7.7 percent to 21.2 percent for most of them between 1965 and 1974. In addition, their generally small populations left major surpluses for investment and considerable wealth for purchasing from abroad.

As can be seen from table 4, Southeast Asian populations were generally larger and per capita wealth smaller than those of the Middle East. However, by the early 1970s, states such as Malaysia, Indonesia, Singapore, and Thailand were achieving political stability and displaying strong economic growth rates, in part due to the ongoing war in Vietnam. Exports of the states of the Association of Southeast Asian States (ASEAN), composed then of Thailand, Malaysia,

Table 3. Major Trading Partners between the Middle East and Southeast Asia, 1963
(in thousands of US$)

	Burma	Cambodia	Mal-Sab-Sar	Singapore	Philippines	Thailand	Vietnam
Imports							
Iran	487	379	3	22,282	619	615	1,088
Sudan	—	11	8	—	150	—	5
UAR	—	727	815	1,124	557	63	21
Exports							
Iran	—	—	—	2,317	16	134	1,204
Sudan	—	—	58	—	—	207	—
UAR	—	—	3,386	2,863	—	75	—

Source: United Nations, *Foreign Trade Statistics of Asia and the Far East* (1963). In addition to these countries, there was also some minor trade with Pakistan, Iraq, Kuwait, Afghanistan, and Egypt, but it tended to be erratic.

Table 4. Population, Per Capita GNP, and Growth Rates: Middle East and Southeast Asia

Country	Population (mid-1974) in millions	Per capita GNP, 1974 (US$)	Growth rates, 1965–74 (%)
Bahrain (est.)	0.25	2,350	21.2 (1971–74)
Iran	33	1,250	7.7
Iraq	10.5	1,110	4.8
Kuwait	0.9	10,030	−2.3
Jordan	2.66	430	−2.5
Oman	0.75	1,660	19.2
Saudi Arabia	8	2,830	9.2
UAE	0.5	11,060	10.4
Brunei (est.)	0.15	6,630	5.7
Indonesia	128	170	4.1
Malaysia	11.5	680	3.8
Philippines	41.5	330	2.7
Singapore	2.2	2,240	10.0
Thailand	40.5	310	4.3

Source: L. Joo-Jack, "West and Southeast Asia: Sharing Common Concerns," 27.

Singapore, Indonesia, and the Philippines, with Brunei joining in the 1980s, had reached approximately US$30 billion by 1975.[18] This was some ten times the amount of total exports and imports from all of Southeast Asia in 1949.[19] Increasingly, these countries also had educated workers who could be attracted to the higher wages offered in the oil-rich states of the Middle East.

By the late 1980s both regions had national economies that were among the stronger systems in Afro-Asia. Because of oil, Saudi Arabia, Kuwait, and the United Arab Emirates (UAE) were among the 24 (out of 121) highest income states of the world. This was also true of Singapore in Southeast Asia, while Thailand, the Philippines, and Malaysia had become middle-income economies. By 1988, imports and exports of the ASEAN states had reached over US$200 billion, and the trade of Saudi Arabia, the UAE, and Kuwait alone was worth approximately US$75 billion.[20]

Southeast Asian political and economic leaders were well aware of the opportunities for trade and investment in West Asia. Many in Malaysia and Indonesia expressed the hope that religious affinity would give their countries a competitive advantage. For the rest of the decade following the oil crisis of 1973, there were major efforts to increase trade and investments. Trade missions flowed back and forth between the two regions. Thus, for two years after 1973, Indonesian trade missions went to Iraq, Kuwait, Egypt, Saudi Arabia, and the UAE; President Suharto of Indonesia went to Egypt, Saudi Arabia, Kuwait, the UAE, Bahrain, and Syria, in part to drum up trade and investment; Prime Minister Tun Abdul Razak of Malaysia was the first of a string of leaders from that country to visit a number of Middle Eastern countries seeking trade and investments. Increasingly, articles appeared in Malaysian publications on how to take advantage of opportunities in the region. In turn, Middle Eastern states, initially led by those from the Persian Gulf, sent teams to Southeast Asia to ascertain the possibility of new investments in the area. Certainly, local chambers of commerce in the Middle East also found these increased opportunities attractive.[21]

A variety of other means were used to develop economic relations. Indonesia, Singapore, and Malaysia began to participate in trade fairs in the Middle East and to hold similar events in their countries to which West Asian representatives were invited. For example, Indonesia was involved in the Cairo Trade Fair on a regular basis and by the early 1980s was participating in trade fairs in Damascus, Izmir, Baghdad, Sharjah, and Jeddah.[22] In 1980–81 alone Indonesia participated in four international trade fairs in the Middle East; held a sole exhibition in Jeddah; did market surveys in Bahrain, Kuwait, and Algeria; sent a timber-selling mission to Kuwait, the UAE, Saudi Arabia, and Egypt; and carried out a number of surveys and mini-fairs at home.[23] In addition, the Indonesian government sponsored a journal, *Iktisadi*, which specifically targeted trade and investment in the Middle East. During the early 1980s Arabs and Saudis formed joint chambers of commerce with local businessmen in Southeast Asia to facilitate trade. In this period business centers were also established by Indonesia and Saudi Arabia in Riyadh and Jakarta. Other examples of cooperative business activities of this nature were a Malaysian-Arab trade and investment conference in Kuala Lumpur in 1987 and the fourth conference of the Islamic Chambers of Commerce and Industry meeting in Jakarta in 1983. The latter was affiliated with the forty-two-member-state Islamic Conference Organization (see chapter 3), and the Indonesians took advantage of the opportunity to sell themselves. They held exhibitions and forums that included local businessmen and organized tours to Indonesian firms.[24]

The Indonesian government developed special organs to seek opportunities in the Middle East. In June 1978 a presidential decree established the Coordinating Team for Export Activities to the Middle East within the Department of Trade and Cooperatives. Aside from membership of functionaries from that ministry, there were "substitute" members representing the ministries of Foreign Affairs, Home Affairs, Justice, Manpower and Transmigration, Public Works, Information, Agriculture, Religious Affairs, Finance, Communication, Defense and Security, Bank Indonesia, and the Investment Board. By 1982 this was supplemented by a Center for Studies on Indonesia and the Middle East. The charge to this team was "coordinating and stimulating as well as supporting the plannings and the measures in utilizing employment and increasing the export of services and goods from Indonesia to the Middle East."[25]

The results of these efforts and opportunities in the decade after 1973 were striking. Trade statistics show this growth. In 1875 all trade by the ASEAN states with Arab nations totaled US$2,596 million in imports and US$367.5 in exports.[26] As indicated in tables 5–7, by 1988 Indonesian exports alone were higher than the earlier ASEAN total.

By the late 1980s trade between the two regions was a significant part of the trade of both areas, although it was still less than each had with the industrialized world. Although the aforementioned statistics do not present these data, Pakistan also became part of the burgeoning two-way trade between Southeast Asia and the Middle East. Thus, Indonesian imports from Pakistan rose from US$13.9 million in 1970 to US$41.5 million in 1979 and exports rose from US$.017 million to US$28.8 million in the same period. Malaysia showed a tenfold growth of exports during the same time.[27] Thailand's exports to the Middle East jumped 33.7 percent between 1972 and 1983.

The major exports to the Middle East have been palm oil, rubber, timber, plywood, tea, coffee, fruits, spices, textiles, and, later, electronics and small manufactured goods.[28] The primary imports to the

Table 5. Indonesian Foreign Trade with the Middle East, 1988
(in millions of US$)

Country	Exports	Imports
Aden	2.479	—
Afghanistan	1.663	2.488
Bahrain	4.0	155.774
Egypt	66.262	3.474
Iran	12.277	39.862
Iraq	7.0	18.575
Jordan	28.317	33.781
Kuwait	34.789	48.952
Lebanon	4.967	1.668
Libya	3.330	168.774
Morocco	21.444	58.174
Oman	7.345	1.470
Qatar	2.373	3.588
Saudi Arabia	170.0	565.19
Syria	3.729	27.085
Tunisia	6.691	25.471
Turkey	3.974	12.963
UAE	86.530	2.031
Yemen	4.244	56.779

Source: Indonesia, Statistik Perdagangan Luar Negiri Indonesia 1988 (Jakarta: Biro Pusal Statisik).

region have been petroleum products, particularly to low producers such as the Philippines, Singapore, and Thailand. However, even Malaysia and Indonesia, petroleum exporters themselves, have imported the high-sulfur, lower-priced oil for domestic use. Other imports have been foodstuffs, textiles, fertilizers, and small manufactures. As is obvious from the tables, there has been a severe overall trade deficit for most Southeast Asian states, largely because of heavy petroleum imports. In addition to data in the tables, other figures show that Singapore had a trade deficit in the first nine months of 1984 of S$7.64 billion to S$1.21 billion; the Philippines in 1982 had a negative trade of US$873 million, although this dropped to US$62 million in 1988; and even Jordan had a positive trade surplus over

Table 6. Malaysian Foreign Trade with the Middle East, 1987
(in 1,000 million ringgit)

Country	Exports	Imports
Algeria	3,793	41
Bahrain	24,250	7,539
Egypt	56,175	3,625
Iran	41,974	4,050
Iraq	129,473	2,428
Jordan	79,541	24,466
Kuwait	19,815	331,384
Lebanon	7,043	108
Libya	234	19
Morocco	5,395	5,330
Oman	22,694	2,317
Qatar	3,813	17,178
Saudi Arabia	210,390	269,570
Sudan	20,487	979
Syria	11,432	33
Tunisia	3,541	6
UAE	?	5,002
Yemen	51,929	—

Source: Malaysia, *Perangkan Padangangan Luar 1987* (Kuala Lumpur: Jabatan
Perangkaan, 1988).

Indonesia in 1985 of US$13 million out of a total trade of only US$47
million.[29]

WORKERS

A major Southeast Asian export to the Middle East starting in the
1970s was workers. The remittances sent back home became a major
source of foreign exchange earnings. Southeast Asian workers were
generally hired for less technical jobs, although some were nurses
and computer operators. Most were unskilled or underskilled construction workers, shop assistants, hospital employees, drivers, me-
chanics, maintenance workers, and ships' crews. They worked on
construction jobs, on pipelines, in hotels, in the oil and gas fields, and

Table 7. Philippine Foreign Trade with the Middle East, 1975 and
1988 (FOB value in US$)

Country	1975	1988
Bahrain	22,386,470	1,231,641
Egypt	1,125,176	3,574,164
Iran	73,500,198	62,623,491
Iraq	26,260,967	1,647,677
Israel	1,874,023	4,112,553
Jordan	4,252	946,329
Kuwait	143,139,224	226,102,242
Libya	44,841	48,068
Morocco	32,354,467	4,915,413
Oman	3,456,474	1,229,884
Qatar	3,965,155	7,983,256
Saudi Arabia	372,810,694	307,470,497
Syria	359,740	488,487

Source: Philippines, 1985 Foreign Trade Statistics of the Philippines (Manila: Philippine
National Census and Statistics Office).

in homes. The high point of Southeast Asian employment in the
Middle East was in the early 1980s before the recession of 1983, although there are serious discrepancies in published figures. For example, estimates of workers from Indonesia, Korea, the Philippines,
and Thailand in 1981 ranged from 116,000 by the World Bank to
713,000 by sources from sending countries.[30] The biggest exporters of
workers were not Muslim countries but the largely Christian Philippines and Buddhist Thailand.[31]

As of the beginning of 1983 one report declared that the Philippines
had 300,000 of its citizens working overseas, accounting for US$1
billion in remittances. Of these, approximately 80 percent were in the
Middle East, a drop from previous levels.[32] A month later another
report put the total in West Asia at 250,000, remitting US$650 mil-
lion.[33] In April 180,000 Filipino workers were said to be in Saudi
Arabia alone, and the Central Bank put remittances from them at
US$800 million.[34] In 1983 Filipino remittances were reported to be
US$955 million, or 21 percent of merchandise exports.[35] There was a
marked increase in remittances that year because of a new law that

workers had to send back at least one-half their basic salaries. These remittances were extremely important to the Philippines, given a deficit of US$360 million in the first three quarters of 1981 alone. In 1989 over 500,000 Filipino workers in the Middle East remitted more than US$2 billion. This figure dropped dramatically after the start of the Gulf War.[36]

In late 1981 there were also an estimated 100,000 to 159,000 Thai workers in the Middle East, primarily in Saudi Arabia, Kuwait, Lebanon, and Iraq. By 1983 the total was given as 277,863 in Saudi Arabia alone.[37] In 1981 Thailand paid US$2.9 billion to import oil from the Middle East. Of that, 17.2 percent (more than U.S.$0.5 billion) came from remittances—more than the value of all but five of Thailand's exports for that year. In the first half of 1983 remittances were US$326.7 million, becoming one of the top three sources of hard currency of the kingdom.[38] When the Iraq-Kuwait conflict broke out in 1990 Thailand was the only Southeast Asian country with a large contingent of workers said to be remaining in those states (6,200 in Iraq and 5,000 in Kuwait).[39] However, there were 200,000 Thais reportedly working in Saudi Arabia in mid-1990.[40]

Of the Muslim states in Southeast Asia, only Indonesia had significant numbers of its people working abroad, considerably fewer than those of the Philippines and Thailand. As of 1982 Indonesia had approximately 42,000 workers in the Middle East, some 22,000 in Saudi Arabia, where they made net monthly incomes of US$484 to US$1,466.[41] Bank of Indonesia figures for 1981 put total remittances at US$32,983,550 and in 1982 at US$38,284,371.[42] The number of Indonesians grew to approximately 100,000 by 1983.

Life was not easy for these workers who lived in unfamiliar surroundings and sent half to three-quarters of their pay home.[43] (On the wall of a clay building in Iraq where some Indonesian workers lived they had written, "For the sake of my family, I shall face the heat and the aridity of nature.") Many workers complained of being cheated by employment agencies (some of which were illegal) and of poor treatment in the Middle East. The non-Muslim workers charged the Saudis in particular of attempting forced conversion to Islam in exchange for stable jobs. Philippine cardinal Sin also complained that Catholics found it difficult to practice their religion in Saudi Arabia.[44] The Thais and Filipinos found the culture of the Middle East difficult to understand, and the ill treatment of workers and execution of some Filipinos for various crimes caused bad publicity for Muslims back home. Criticism of living and working conditions did not only come from non-Muslims, as even Malaysians expressed their unhappiness.

INVESTMENTS

Any cursory review of the financial pages of Southeast Asian newspapers during the fifteen years after 1973 will show the large number of investment activities engaged in by Middle Eastern financial institutions. The following material does not make a complete list, but it illustrates the variety of economic agreements.

Kuwait

1975   Kuwaiti finance team goes to Indonesia.

1976   Kuwait loans M$60 million to FELDA.

1977   Kuwait to be biggest underwriter in the construction of a US$700 million Batam refinery.

1978   Kuwait Fund for Arab Economic Development (KFAED) agrees to M$42 million toward Trengganu River dam project, M$72 million for Palong rubber scheme project, and M$48 million for oil palm production. Caps three years in which Kuwait has loaned over M$1,120 million.

1979   Kuwait finalizes plan for M$100 million joint venture in Sabah timber.

1980   Plans arranged for Kuwaiti-Malaysian investment holding company.
        Kuwait to take 20 percent equity Petronas refining plant in Malacca.

1981   KFAED provides US$60 million for Jakarta Cikampek highway project on soft terms. Later in the eighties KFAED approves a series of projects in both Malaysia and government-owned Kuwait Real Estate Investment Consortium was active in Singapore.

Saudi Arabia

1974   Saudis pledge first aid to Indonesia and support second five-year plan.

1975   M$180 million loan from Saudis primarily for medical faculty at Universiti Kebangsaan, Malaysia. Indonesia receives a US$100 million loan for development projects.

1976   M$183 from Saudi Fund for Development for development proj-
        ects in Malaysia and US$76 million in loans to Indonesia for a
        fertilizer project.

1977   Saudis advance Indonesia US$50 million for road projects.

1982   Saudis aid thirteen development projects, with M$400 million for
        Malaysian fourth five-year plan.

1985   Saudis provide aid to flood-control project in Acheh, Indonesia,
        and US$25.6 million for palm oil project.

1986   Saudi Development Fund allocates M$132 for Penang port and
        East-West highway in Malaysia.

Other States

1974   Gulf states send investment team to Indonesia.

1975   Abu Dhabi Economic Development Fund provides M$150 million
        for cement plant in Malaysia.
        Iran provides Indonesia with a US$200 million loan for fertilizer
        plant in West Java.

1976   Same fund provides "soft loan" of M$21 million for two develop-
        ment projects in Sabah and Sarawak.

1977   Abu Dhabi to support Sarawak projects on paper, palm oil, ce-
        ment, etc., at M$200 million.

1980   Bank of Abu Dhabi makes S$28 million loan to purchase five
        vessels.

Multinational Financial Institutions

Aside from these bilateral efforts, a number of multilateral projects
have been based on groups of banks or states. Two examples should
suffice. In 1979 a M$220 million ten-year loan for Malaysia was syndi-
cated by twenty-four banks and managed by the Arab Malaysian
Development Bank. It was publicized as the first inflow of private
petrodollars into the country.[45] A similar syndicate of West Asian
banks agreed to provide the Philippines with US$500 million in re-
volving credit to finance oil imports. This syndicate was headed by
the Saudi National Commercial Bank.[46]

The Islamic Development Bank, established in 1975, is owned by
members of the Organization of Islamic Conference (OIC), including
Malaysia and Indonesia. Funds are to be used to finance foreign trade
and other projects. Generally, loans are to be guaranteed by the indi-

vidual or central bank. As of 1982, only US$38.3 million was provided to Indonesia for four projects.[47] Malaysia also received loans during that period for such projects as a fertilizer plant and credit for the Malaysian Development Bank.

Despite this long list of projects and loans, the total amount of actual Middle Eastern investments in Southeast Asian states has been relatively low. Most of what has been provided has been in the form of loans, albeit often at good rates. However, even the total amount of loans was only a small percentage of the amount distributed throughout the world. For example, in only the first quarter of 1983 the seven Arab development agencies allocated US$493.46 to the Third World, which included thirty-four loans to thirty-one countries.[48] The Arabs proved to be cautious when it came to investing in Southeast Asian industry rather than property and markets. In the decade after 1973, their preference was to look to North America and Western Europe, and even there investment tended to be in U.S. Treasury notes and other securities rather than direct investment. Arab entrepreneurs had been bitten once in the early 1960s when they entered the U.S. stock market, with unfortunate results.[49] To them, the West Asian region was something of a terra incognito, and this unfamiliarity was a major barrier to funding.

A good example of Arab thinking was displayed at a seminar on investment by Arab oil producers held under the auspices of the Arab Planning Institute in 1974.[50] The conference was predicated on the expectation of a surplus of over US$100 billion in the next seven years. A series of problems concerning the expansion of investment was noted, including a shortage of human resources, a serious lack of agencies to evaluate projects, a dearth of external contacts with outside resources, and an absence of cooperation with development finance institutions.[51]

Thus, the total of direct foreign investment by West Asians has been significantly lower than that from Japan and Taiwan in Asia, Western Europe, and the United States. Admittedly, it is often difficult to ascertain exact amounts of private and government investments in these regions. However, some data are available. An analysis of foreign investment in Indonesia from 1967 to 1986 showed no Middle Eastern state among the top twenty-seven investing countries.[52] Except for real estate, such as the Marina Center, the Middle

East was not an early major player in Singapore. At an Arab-Malaysian forum held in 1987 to discuss financial ties between the two regions, the relatively small amount of Arab investment in neighboring Malaysia also became clear.[53] The conference underscored the difficulty in obtaining Arab investment information, in part due to the multiplicity of sources of funding. The Malaysian secretary-general of trade and industry, Datuk Ahmad Sarji Abdul Hamid, disclosed that approval had been obtained from the Malaysian Development Authority (MIDA) for only fourteen manufacturing projects of distinct Arab origin. Investments were in building material, textiles, engineering and chemical companies, and electrical products. These had a combined paid-up capital of only M$32.1 million.[54] This does not mean that there have been no Middle Eastern investments in the region, but they have tended to be small.[55]

There have also been some Southeast Asian financial activities in the Middle East, particularly in the construction field. For example, in early 1981 it was announced that by the end of that year Indonesian construction contractors would have won US$1 billion in contracts from Saudi Arabia, including such projects as the Jubail Naval Base, KAMA II, and the Peace Sun Air Force contract. In addition, Indonesians were involved in major construction projects dealing with installing telephone exchanges, road construction, computers, etc.[56] Similarly, Philippine construction firms have been concerned with projects about bridges, airports, and seaports.

CONCLUSION

We can now return to the question of whether there has been any relationship between the religious affinity of Muslim states in Southeast Asia and the Middle East and economic actions. Obvious examples of gifts and loans for specific religious purposes have already been noted. These have been of considerable importance and in the aggregate have strengthened Islamic institutions through aid to mosques and religious organizations. This assistance was augmented over time with the increased wealth of Middle Eastern states. However, there has been no clear propensity to hire workers for Middle Eastern projects primarily from Muslim countries in Southeast Asia. In fact, the largest numbers of foreign workers came from Buddhist

Thailand and the Christian Philippines, and there is no evidence that special consideration was given Muslim minorities in those countries.

What then of trade and investment? In the initial years after the 1973 oil crisis and economic boom in the Middle East there were many, perhaps naive, expressions of hope that Muslim states in Southeast Asia would benefit inordinately. (They had received priority treatment in terms of petroleum imports during the 1973 boycott.) There were also expectations that involvement in the economic organs of the OIC would prove useful, and Indonesian and Malaysian speakers at Islamic forums emphasized the importance of unity and mutual economic cooperation among Muslim states. In some cases religion *has* appeared to influence Saudi economic policy decisions. For instance, there was a report in 1977 that a Saudi housing contract in Malaysia had a requirement that there be only Muslim workers,[57] but it was later denied. The Saudis also restricted oil exports to the Philippines in 1981 because of alleged mistreatment of Filipino Muslims. After Imelda Marcos, wife of President Ferdinand Marcos, went to New York City to talk to Saudi representatives, the cutoff was halted.[58]

However, over time, Southeast Asians have found that the Arabs have been much more interested in the financial benefits of overseas projects. As the director of the Arab-Malaysian Development Bank commented, the original optimistic view of the role of religion was a misconception. He said, "Arab industrialists are hard-headed businessmen. When it comes to paying out money, they take out their little Japanese calculators and do their sums."[59] In 1985, Kirdi Dipoyudo wrote that "[the Arabs'] foreign investment is based on the business principle to gain the largest possible amount of profit."[60] Again, the aforementioned Arab-Malaysian forum held in 1987 reinforced the Malaysians' view that economic factors were paramount. The author of the article in *Malaysian Business* remarked, "As is well known, the Arabs can prove particularly hard-nosed when it comes to business."[61] This article, as well as many others published earlier, deplored the inability of Southeast Asians to take advantage of opportunities in the Middle East. At no time in the accounts of the 1987 meeting was any comment published regarding religious affinity, nor has it been given prominence in any of the other business-trade periodicals published in Southeast Asia. The aforementioned 1974 meeting in the Middle East concerning how to spend petrodollars never considered religion as a factor in where to invest. Almost all the commentators at the seminar stressed the need for hard-headed economic analysis.[62] In sum, with a few minor exceptions, the bottom line appears to have been the bottom line.

Chapter 3

POLITICAL INTERACTION

 This chapter is an assessment of political interaction between Southeast Asia and the Middle East. The chapter is divided into four sections: the development of formal diplomatic relations; Southeast Asian involvement in Middle Eastern issues; Middle Eastern interest in Southeast Asian political questions; and Southeast Asian participation in international Islamic organizations. However, it should be noted initially that any analysis of political activity between Southeast Asia and the Middle East presents certain methodological problems.

Assessing the extent to which rhetoric is an accurate reflection of policy presents a generic difficulty. For example, what do protestations of Islamic brotherhood mean in actual practice? Are some foreign policy statements issued for domestic political purposes alone? Of particular concern in this analysis are allegations that Southeast Asian governments have consciously made false charges that certain Middle Eastern states have illicitly intervened in Southeast Asian internal politics. It is not always possible to prove the veracity of such accusations, particularly in systems where the press is controlled. In addition, the frequent absence of accurate polling techniques or fully democratic expression makes it difficult both to assess the depth of public opinion on any given issue and the extent to which those in power may be reacting to the popular will. For example, how should we consider demonstrations against attacks on Iraq in early 1991 by the U.S.-led coalition? Did they reflect widespread support of the Iraqi regime or popular expressions of Islamic solidarity, or was this an example of a small, highly motivated minority?

It is essential that the observer recognizes how domestic forces have influenced the foreign policies of Southeast Asian states toward the Middle East. Indonesian and Malaysian politics, especially as they have related to domestic religious opposition, illustrate the importance of this interaction.[1]

Since its declaration of independence in 1945, Indonesia's governing elite has tended to reflect secular rather than Islamic values. Under President Sukarno, political power was primarily in the hands of those who sought to contain the role of religion to personal belief and to keep it from influencing domestic and foreign policy. Although Indonesia was and is 90 percent Muslim, these political leaders were predominantly from that Javanese population that reflected the island's more syncretic and mystical Islamic beliefs. They were desirous of containing the influence of the more "orthodox" Muslims who sought a greater role for Islam in the country's social and political life. As the late President Sukarno and the Indonesian Communist Party (PKI) drew closer together during the early 1960s and Muslim organizations became more alienated from Jakarta's foreign and domestic goals, the rift between secular and religious elements became ever wider.

After Suharto and the military gained power in the mid-1960s, Muslim organizations hoped for a greater role in Indonesian politics, partly due to their activities in eliminating the Communists after the abortive 1965 coup. However, when the military realized that these Muslim organizations had their own agendas and were the only sizable organized resistance to military rule, Jakarta followed much the same policy as previously, of attempting to control Muslim political power.

Through much of the 1980s there were increasingly serious tensions between elements of the Muslim community and the government of President Suharto. Difficulties arose from perceptions within Muslim political and religious organizations that those in power did not reflect proper Islamic values, that they had been polluted by Western economic and cultural influences, that they had not displayed sufficient interest in the economic and social problems of rural Muslims, and that they were attempting to foster un-Islamic ideologies. The major complaint during this period was the government's insistence on pressing the ideology of the Panchasila (or Pantja Sila, Five Principles) on these organizations.

Originally championed by President Sukarno as the ideological foundation of his regime, the Panchasila also became the basis of Suharto's ideology. Overall, it received little criticism from the Muslims with the exception of the fifth principle. As first articulated by Sukarno, the offensive principle declared, "The principle of Belief in God! Not only should the Indonesian people believe in God, but every Indonesian should believe in his own God. The Christian should worship God according to the teachings of Jesus Christ, Moslems according to the teachings of the Prophet Mohammad, Buddhists should perform their religious ceremonies in accordance with the books they have."[2]

To many Muslims, this formulation appeared to be at best agnosticism. When the Suharto regime called for the Panchasila to be the sole ideology of all organizations, many objected strenuously. This resistance raised levels of tension among the Muslims and helped to underscore governmental suspicions of all Islamic political activities. The fear of undesirable influences such as the Iranian Revolution and radical Middle Eastern movements only reinforced negative attitudes within the Suharto regime.

Since the deposition of President Sukarno in the late 1960s, the only strongly organized opposition to the Suharto government has come from dissatisfied Muslims. During the 1980s, the leadership of the public Muslim organizations generally favored peaceful opposition and even largely withdrew from politics, but some elements had more restive groups and individuals. From these fringes developed small, violent elements accused of bombings, arson, and plane hijackings. In addition, some religious teachers used Islam to launch oral attacks on what they perceived to be a corrupt and un-Islamic regime. To meet this challenge, the authorities sought to weaken Islamic political influence by diluting Muslim party power, meting out severe sentences to those preaching what were termed seditious attacks on the government, and underscoring dangers of "deviant" Islam. While these tensions had decreased by the end of the 1980s, they were particularly prevalent during the era when the Iranian Revolution appeared to be most contagious.

Malaysia is a limited parliamentary democracy in which religion and ethnicity have defined much of political life. The centerpiece of the party system has been the Alliance (later expanded to become the

National Front), a multiracial coalition that has dominated national and most state politics since independence in the mid-1950s. The Alliance/National Front has been headed by a Muslim Malay party, the United Malay National Organization (UMNO), since independence. UMNO has produced all of the country's prime ministers and most of its senior ministers since that time. If Malaysia's democracy has been limited by an overly liberal use of antisedition laws and limits on speech regarding race and religion, UMNO politics can nevertheless be described as among the most democratic in the Third World. The primary Muslim opposition to UMNO comes from the Parti Islam sa-Malaysia (PAS), whose leadership has continuously emphasized traditional Malay and Muslim values. It has been incumbent on UMNO to maintain a pluralistic racial policy to meet the expectations of the multiracial coalition it heads while attempting to satisfy its own Muslim party membership and to forestall possible inroads from PAS.[3]

UMNO's need to appeal to its Muslim constituency has been one of the reasons for the government's efforts to support Islamic causes at home and abroad. However, the Malaysian regime sees a danger in what it believes to be extremist interpretations of Islam. These fears arise from the more radical stance on Islamic issues held by PAS and some UMNO constituents and the infrequent cases of even more radical groups using violence against the government. Thus, like those in power in Jakarta, National Front leaders in Kuala Lumpur have constantly stressed the dangers of deviant Islam. It is within these contexts that the interaction of both governments with the Middle East must be understood. In sum, Jakarta has sought to downplay the role of Islam in its foreign policy, and Malaysia has sought to emphasize its Islamic credentials. At the same time, both have attempted to ensure that more radical Islamic influences are contained.

DIPLOMATIC RELATIONS

Many Southeast Asian countries did not achieve independence until long after World War II. Thus, formal diplomatic relations between the Middle East and Southeast Asia are a postwar phenomenon. Although Thailand has remained independent in modern times and the Philippines became free in 1946, other states with large Muslim populations became free much later. Indonesia formally gained independence in 1949 (it declared its freedom in 1945), Malaysia in 1957, and Brunei in 1984. Both the Philippines and Thailand opened formal relations with Middle Eastern states at an early date. Thailand had diplomatic relations with seven states as early as 1961 (Afghanistan, Iran, Iraq, Lebanon, Pakistan, the United Arab Republic [UAR], and Turkey), but as of the mid-1980s had only increased that number by two (adding Israel, Oman, and Jordan and dropping Afghanistan). In the late 1950s the Philippines had shown considerable public sympathy for Israel and expressed common bonds of democracy.[4] However, twenty years later, the Philippines showed increasing official sympathy for the Arabs and had relations with about half the world's Muslim states, with resident embassies in Iran, Pakistan, Egypt, Kuwait, Libya, Saudi Arabia, the UAE, and Morocco.[5] In the 1970s, during the early years of the Marcos regime, the Philippine government developed an aggressive campaign to improve relations with Muslim countries. This was based on the perceived need to ease tensions with the Muslim world because of the Moro problem and forestall criticism of Manila's policies against its own Muslim people. In this period the Philippines opened diplomatic relations with an average of three Muslim countries a year, in spite of the large financial burden this placed on a weakened economy.

The major Muslim states of Southeast Asia were slow to open diplomatic relations with the Middle East after the end of colonial rule. Five years after independence Malaysia had embassies only in the Muslim states of Indonesia, Pakistan, and the UAR. This number increased to eight in 1967 and to a dozen in 1984. By 1991 there were formal relations and embassies with almost every Middle Eastern country. In part, the delay in developing these contacts can be laid to the earlier Malaysian concentration on its traditional British interests and its involvement in local Southeast Asian issues. However, it was because of the latter, particularly the need to develop support for its position in the conflict with Indonesia in the early 1960s, that efforts were exerted to increase relations with the Middle East. Later expansion of relations rose out of a combination of the growing economic ties noted in chapter 2 and Malaysia's increased involvement in domestic and international Islamic issues.

Indonesia initially worked actively to develop relations with the

Middle East during its fight for independence in the late 1940s. In 1946, Egypt, followed by other Arab states, declared that the Indonesians were no longer subjects of the Dutch. The Arab League also took a strong pro-Indonesian position and recommended that all Arab states recognize the new republic. After an exchange of visits of Egyptian and Indonesian representatives, a diplomatic mission was established in Cairo in 1947.[6] Michael Leifer has termed this "part of a general diplomatic strategy designed to secure recognition and international endorsement for the embattled Republic."[7] Leifer also argues that this was "the only period in which Islam has served as a positive element in foreign policy."[8] In the years that followed, the Middle East was not a prime area of interest for President Sukarno. As his policies became increasingly oriented toward an anticapitalist, anti-imperialist position, he found little in common with some of the more conservative Middle Eastern states. While his successor, President Suharto, has also not emphasized Middle Eastern relations, there has been a gradual expansion of formal diplomatic relations with the Middle East. Indonesia increased its diplomatic ties with that region from nine states in 1970 to fourteen in the mid-1980s.

Thus, by 1991 Southeast Asian states with sizable Muslim populations had established formal diplomatic relations with all the major Middle Eastern states, although financial contingencies at times meant that residential embassies were not to be found in all countries. Frequently a diplomat served more than one capital or residencies were small. Where there were major economic interests or large numbers of workers or students, the embassy staff was likely to be more active. For their part, states with Muslim minorities had extensive relations with the Muslim world in part because of their longstanding independence and in part because of the perceived need to assuage criticisms of their treatment of their indigenous Islamic populace.

SOUTHEAST ASIAN INTERESTS IN THE MIDDLE EAST

As noted in chapter 1, prewar involvement of Southeast Asians in Middle Eastern political issues was primarily confined to the caliphate question, and the absence of independence in both regions severely limited the degree to which any concerted influence could be brought to bear. This pattern changed significantly after the war, in part because of the normal expansion of international relations that came with independence, particularly the involvement of these new states in Third World activities. As we shall see, Southeast Asian states interacted with their Middle Eastern brethren in the United Nations, nonaligned organizations, economic groups, and Islamic associations.

However, there were particular Southeast Asian factors that came to play an expanding role in the Middle East. Countries that had Muslim minorities in conflict with the central government, such as Burma, Thailand, and the Philippines, came under considerable pressure from Muslim states to treat their Islamic minorities more equitably. This move, in turn, increased these countries' awareness of Middle Eastern matters and made them more willing to express their support of Islamic goals concerning such issues as Israel and Afghanistan.

Domestic forces in Southeast Asia also had their role. The growth of the Islamic resurgence in the region caused local pressure for governments to become more involved in worldwide Muslim issues. With the expansion of communications, events such as the attacks in the sacred sites of Mecca, the Gulf War, the Iranian Revolution, and the intifada readily evoked reactions from the public in Kuala Lumpur and Jakarta.

Although somewhat difficult to support with hard evidence, there also appear to have been different views on the importance of the Middle East and attitudes toward Arabs. The Malays have tended to be more attracted to the Middle East in the postindependence period than other Southeast Asian entities. Perhaps as a small country, Malaysia obtains a sense of being a player in a wider field by involving itself in Middle Eastern affairs. As well, the more religious tone of Malaysian politics has led to a closer identification with all Muslims. On the other hand, as the world's largest Muslim nation, Indonesians feel that they are a power unto themselves, and there is some bitterness regarding what they see as Arab expressions of superiority over Southeast Asian Muslims. During the Suharto years, there has also been much more concentration on regional issues, and the Middle East has been perceived as a quagmire, both domestically and internationally. So the Middle East has not held the centrality in Indonesia's foreign policy that it has in Malaysia's.

A subtle difference exists with regard to attitudes toward Arabs. In both countries there is some negative reaction to Arabs, particularly regarding their perceived attitudes of superiority and their emphasis on money. Observers such as G. Hein and F. Weinstein and my own interviews have elicited strong statements from elite Indonesian spokesmen about the arrogance and materialism of the Arabs.[9] Interviews and articles collected by Hein provided statements such as "They always change sides: one minute they're fighting and the next minute they're kissing and hugging each other"; "Arabs are unstable and can't be trusted. Plus, they are culturally different than Indonesians"; "We are better Muslims than those in most Arab countries. We do not drink"; and "It is certainly true that Indonesians are not particularly fond of Arabs. But then it must also be asked: Do Indonesians really like any foreigners?"[10] Although such statements may also be heard in Malaysia, there is a somewhat greater appreciation of Arab culture and language there and certainly more care among officials in criticizing the Arabs. Still, one often hears private assertions about the character of local Arabs that are not particularly flattering.

Finally, even given these negative views, there has been an increasing sense of being part of the *ummah*. Improved communications and travel have given it greater impetus. The increased sense of belonging has also meant that many Southeast Asian Muslims believe that they have a natural role to play in Islamic questions in other regions. Different governments have looked at this differently, but their citizens have put constant pressure upon them to react to conditions in other Muslim societies. These factors can be elucidated by looking in depth at four Middle Eastern issues: Israel, the Iranian Revolution (which will be covered separately in chapter 4), the Soviet invasion of Afghanistan, and conflicts between Middle Eastern states.

Israel

Policies of Southeast Asian states toward Israel and the Palestinian issue have varied over time and place. Over time, there has been a gradual growth in public criticism of Israel's policies toward the Palestinians and increased support of the Palestinians in terms of their demands for self-determination. For states with Muslim minorities, such as the Philippines and Thailand, criticism has been based, at least in part, on the desire to mitigate Muslim criticism of treatment of their own minorities and to ensure continued supplies of petroleum products. But overall sympathy for the Palestinian cause has not led to a break in diplomatic relations between Israel and any Muslim minority state.

Malaysia has been the most vociferous critic of Israel in Southeast Asia, but it was not always so. In the first decade after independence, attacks on Israeli policies were rather muted, and the government of Tengku Abdul Rahman was content with mild criticism. For example, a review of the speech of Deputy Prime Minister Tun Razak before the General Assembly of the United Nations in September 1966 finds the Malaysian government far more interested in South Africa, Vietnam, and Taiwan.[11]

However, particularly after the 1967 Arab-Israeli War, Malaysian policy became increasingly critical of Israel. In the 1970s Tengku, as the first secretary-general of the OIC, and Malaysian representatives at the OIC meetings of heads of state and conferences of the Islamic foreign ministers, and the United Nations demanded the return of Arab lands and called for Muslim solidarity against Israel. A statement by Foreign Minister Tengku Ahmad Rithauddeen at the 1977 Islamic Conference of Foreign Ministers defines what has been the Malaysian policy since the late 1960s.

> The forces of Zionism, and Israeli aggression and territorial aggrandizement, in complete disregard of world public opinion and resolutions of the United Nations continues to pose as a threat to peace in the Middle East with serious implication to international security and stability. Peace in the Middle East can be guaranteed only by two conditions, that is the total withdrawal of Israel from its illegal occupation of Arab territories including Holy Jerusalem which it has taken by force, and a just solution to the very Palestinian issue whose fundamental and basic question, including that of a Palestinian state be solved.[12]

To underscore its position, Israelis have been forbidden to enter Malaysia and visas were refused to Israelis for international events such as the World Badminton Federation games held in Kuala Lumpur in 1977.[13]

Then and since, the Kuala Lumpur government and Muslim political and religious organizations have attacked a wide range of Israeli actions, from the rescue attempt at Entebbe to the bombing of PLO headquarters in Tunis. Prime Minister Mahathir called the latter act "despicable" and declared that "Israel is becoming a menace internationally and we must all work together to condemn and punish Israel."[14] Malaysia annually joins other Muslim nations in observing Al-Aqsa Day on August 21, which commemorates the perceived Israeli sacrilege of the Al-Aqsa Mosque. That day is also one of expressing solidarity with the Palestinian people and condemning Israeli policies such as the "Judaizing of the Holy City by changing its demographic and cultural character."[15]

Under Mahathir, Malaysia has taken an even stronger position against what it perceives to be a totally unacceptable situation in the Occupied Territories. Malaysia hosted the Asian Regional Conference on the Question of Palestine in 1983, where it took a leading role in committing the meeting to the Palestinian cause. The prime minister has been particularly vigorous in his rhetoric against Zionism. He has criticized the treatment of Palestinians by Zionists, declaring that "all men of goodwill must abhor this mass persecution perpetrated by people who craved the sympathy of the world when they were persecuted but are no better than their former persecutors when they have the power."[16] When his government has been criticized, he has questioned whether international publications are the tools of Zionists and has accused Zionists of attempting to destroy both Malaysia and Islam.[17]

Malaysia was also an early supporter of the PLO. In October 1981 it became the first Asian country to recognize the PLO and later gave it full diplomatic status. It also supported full PLO diplomatic representation at the United Nations.[18] Yassir Arafat has visited Malaysia where he has spoken before the Parliament and been hosted at a banquet given by the paramount ruler. Local organizations such as ABIM have given money to the PLO, and a Palestinian Solidarity Fund was established. More than once PLO representatives have given copious praise to Malaysia for its support of the movement.[19] In sum, Malaysia has become the Palestinians' best friend and Israel's most vocal critic in Asia.

Indonesia's policies have been more complex. From the time of independence, Jakarta has officially supported the Arab cause, including the unconditional withdrawal of Israel from the Occupied

Territories and the right of the Palestinians to have an independent state.[20] In the words of Suharto, "Our attitude has always been clear from the beginning, that is, we stand on the side of the Arab peoples and that of the people of Palestine who are fighting for their just rights against the arrogant aggression of Israel."[21] During the Sukarno years, Israel was excluded from the Asian Games. This action led to problems with the Olympics Committee, and, interestingly enough, there was no real backing of Indonesia's stand from Arab states. Under Suharto, Indonesia has told the United Nations that "the aggression by Israel against the neighboring countries has caused death and incomparable destruction"[22] and joined in naming 1984 the "Year of Palestine."

However, this public rhetoric has hidden fundamental differences between the policies of Malaysia and Indonesia. First, since the days of Sukarno, Jakarta has tended to present its criticism of Israel in antiimperialist rather than anti-Islamic terms. As Weinstein commented, "For Sukarno, Israel was an outpost of Western imperialism in the Asian-African world."[23] On his part, Suharto has also tended to avoid religious factors in defining Jakarta's position.

Second, under Sukarno, and particularly since Suharto's rise to power, Indonesia has preached moderation to the Arab states in their dealings with Israel. Thus, it cautioned against a lengthy boycott in 1973, noting that it could backfire, raise prices in Middle Eastern states, and be commercially disadvantageous to Indonesia.[24] Indonesia sent troops to the UN peacekeeping force in 1973 as it had previously done in Gaza. Jakarta ultimately remained neutral with regard to the Camp David Accords and, as we shall see, did not condemn Egypt for its role in the agreements. Vice-President A. Malik noted that the "part of the Arab struggle that has been achieved by President Sadat is good."[25] And despite years of lobbying by Muslim groups in Indonesia and frequent expectations of changed government policy, PLO leader Arafat did not visit Jakarta for the first time until July 1984. At that time, the Suharto government promised that the PLO could set up a bureau, and Arafat was careful to underscore that his organization was not an Islamic movement but was pluralist in religious composition.[26] Indonesia had been willing to give diplomatic support to the PLO in the United Nations but has worried about its having an office on Indonesian soil. In part it was a religious concern, but Jakarta was also particularly wary during the 1960s and 1970s about PLO ties to communist and other radical organizations and governments. Again, rhetoric tended to be victorious over action. This rather cautious line of policy not only reflected worry over domestic religious issues but also resulted from differences within the ruling elite about both Israel and the Arabs. There has been general agreement that the Arabs have been unrealistic in their belief that they could defeat the Israelis militarily. Elements within the Indonesian armed forces have expressed worry about previous Arab ties to communist states and have shown admiration for Israeli military and development capabilities. Materially, in 1979 the Indonesian purchased fourteen Israeli fighter aircraft.[27] Rhetorically, as one army leader stated, "When we speak privately among ourselves, we cannot help admiring what the Israelis have done, though we feel bound to support the Arabs. We do feel it was wrong to establish Israel, but that question aside, they have provided an excellent example of what a nation can do by hard work. They have done a marvelous job of economic development."[28]

Beyond this aspect there has not been much consensus on the bases for Indonesia's policies toward Israel. Secular nationalists of the Sukarno era and contemporary governing elites have displayed rather tepid support for the Arabs, basing their oratory at least in part on anti-imperialist assumptions. This support has been tempered by negative stereotypes regarding Arab capabilities, the desire to downplay religious issues, and a sense that this issue has not been central to Indonesian foreign policy goals. In recent years, the government has displayed somewhat greater allegiance to the Palestinian cause. This reflects a more accommodating relationship with its Muslim constituents as well as local reactions to the intifada and Israeli treatment of the Palestinians.

A more continuous and unambiguous policy of antipathy to Israel has come from nongovernmental Muslim organizations. A review of Islamic journals and newspapers shows greater attention to the religious connection than found in government pronouncements. Nor have comments been as moderate when it comes to Israeli treatment of Palestinians, the occupation of Jerusalem, and Israeli attacks on Arab interests. Events of the late 1980s and early 1990s have led to even stronger reactions. Given the withdrawal of Soviet power from the Middle East, Indonesian Muslims are also no longer so troubled about the relationship of Arab governments to communism.

In sum, official Indonesia has publicly supported main-line Third World condemnation of Israeli actions but has not stood at the forefront of these critics, nor has it underscored Islam as a factor in its decision to support the Arab cause. At the same time, domestic Islamic organizations have more clearly mirrored Malaysian views.

Afghanistan

The movement of the Soviet Union into Afghanistan in 1979 was viewed by many Muslims in Southeast Asia as an attack on Islam. The rhetoric of the mujahidin attacking godless communism and articulating its goals in the name of religion reinforced this attitude. Again, Indonesia, while vigorously condemning the actions of the Soviets, formulated its opposition to the presence of the Soviets in Afghanistan primarily in terms of criticism of unacceptable imperialist actions rather than the defense of Islam. This official position was not mirrored in statements by Islamic organizations. Both Muslim political and religious spokesmen of these organizations called the Soviet invasion a war against Muslim peoples as well as a danger to world peace.

Malaysian authorities, on the other hand, formulated their criticism in more Islamic terms, although they also condemned the Soviet actions as a challenge to the Third World. Kuala Lumpur joined with the OIC in calling for the withdrawal of the Soviets and refused to attend the Olympic Games in Moscow in 1980. The Malaysian government also donated M$150,000 for the Afghan refugees and agreed to allow the mujahidin to open an office in Kuala Lumpur (the UMNO youth offered a building free of charge).[29] Deputy Prime Minister Mahathir told the Third Islamic Summit Conference in 1981 that "We have seen Muslim countries swallowed up by the Communists and the children of conquered Muslims separated from their faith. The chances are very real that unless we can really help, in one or two generations the Afghans may no longer be Muslims, may be completely lost to Islam."[30] At the same time the government attempted to contain demonstrations by nongovernmental organizations, apparently to keep them from making political capital from such efforts. An interesting aspect of this was that when Anwar Ibrahim was president of a *dak-wah* organization, ABIM (an Islamic outreach group), which was held in suspicion by the government, he was blocked from leading a mass demonstration in opposition to the Soviets. After he was coopted into the government, one of his first activities was to lead an official gathering with similar sympathies.

Intra–Middle Eastern Disputes

Prior to World War II, the caliphate question was the only issue in the Middle East in which Southeast Asian Muslims were deeply involved. Three postwar conflicts among Muslim states in the Middle East came to the particular attention of Southeast Asian governments: the ostracism of Egypt after Camp David, the Iran-Iraq War, and the occupation of Kuwait by the Iraqis. In each of these cases there was a strong desire in both Kuala Lumpur and Jakarta to see a peaceful negotiation of divisions between Muslims, and both held the view that such disputes could only help the enemies of Islam and the Third World. These were not the only disputes in which these Southeast Asian states have been involved. For example, the Indonesian ambassador to the United Nations helped to ease the conflict between Turkey and Syria in the mid-1950s,[31] and Jakarta and other Southeast Asian capitals took strong positions in favor of independence for North African states, although not always on the basis of being Muslim coreligionists.

Indonesia and Malaysia did not agree with the effort to ostracize Egypt following its acceptance of the Camp David Accords. Indonesia was careful not to condemn either Egypt or the accords publicly and, in fact, showed some acceptance of the ideas developed at Camp David. Sadat's early efforts were met with some sympathy and, after Egypt came under attack from Arab hard-liners, Jakarta neither broke off diplomatic relations nor joined in the condemnation of Cairo. Hein reports that in 130 interviews he conducted from 1979 to 1984 with foreign policy elites, no one showed outright disapproval of the basic tenets of the Camp David Accords.[32]

At the same time, Jakarta did not want to antagonize Arab opinion and did not attempt to lead efforts to support the Sadat decision. As one of the Muslim leaders interviewed by Hein stated, "There is a special relationship with Egypt and we actually support Camp David, but unfortunately we can't do so publicly." A retired Foreign Ministry expert on the Middle East reiterated this view, stating that "we shouldn't get more involved now, because we would just make enemies."[33] Several interviewees, in fact, criticized the government for not supporting Cairo's efforts. Malaysia generally mirrored Indonesia's unwillingness to condemn Egypt, although it was apparently less supportive of the tenets of Camp David. Kuala Lumpur was even more worried about divisions within the Islamic community and desirous of mediating tensions among the contending parties.

The Iran-Iraq conflict brought similar reactions, as both Southeast Asian countries called for a peaceful settlement and deplored divisions in the Middle East. Again, both attempted to display their neutrality, and Malaysia was more active in offers to help with mediation. Malaysia was a member of the seven-nation peace committee appointed by the OIC to endeavor to achieve peace in the conflict. Throughout the war there was an effort to maintain relations as usual with both parties. As noted, the conflict did lead to a major decline in trade relations but not because of political decisions made in Southeast Asia.

The Iraqi occupation of Kuwait and UN actions against Baghdad brought Malaysia into the forefront of the issues involved since it was a member of the Security Council during this period. While there were public demonstrations against coalition military force, Malaysia did support the initial Security Council boycott vote and the later agreement that force could be used against Iraq. However, the level of power used brought strong reactions from the government. Prime Minister Mahathir accused the United States of hiding the degree of destruction of Iraq and of trying to destroy that country.[34]

Indonesia also supported the UN resolutions, although it was torn between past loyalties to both Iraq and Kuwait. Foreign Minister Ali Alatas described the annexation of Kuwait as establishing bad precedents for the developing world.[35] The Foreign Ministry supported the UN resolution opposing Iraqi aggression and the Security Council resolution to allow the use of force. However, Jakarta did not accept the Saudi proposal to join the multinational military forces. As in Malaysia, there was considerable local criticism of U.S. policies and its military presence in the gulf. Muslim organizations in both countries were attracted to Saddam Hussein's articulation of Palestinian rights and the "double standard" used by the United States regarding Iraq and Israel. This attitude was also expressed by Muslims in the Philippines, Singapore, and Thailand, although it was by no means a unanimous view.[36] Publicly, both Singapore and Thai authorities strongly backed the coalition forces and criticized Iraq's actions in Kuwait.

In numerous interviews reported in the local and international press, many Muslims argued that it was better to support a bad Muslim government against non-Muslim antagonists.[37] Others were deeply influenced by the possible involvement of or aid to Israel. These views were reinforced by a general lack of sympathy for wealthy Kuwait and Saudi Arabia and memories of the perceived lack of sensitivity of the Saudis following the death of many Indonesians in the 1990 tunnel stampede in Mecca.

In each of the three issues, the governments in Southeast Asia were concerned with divisiveness in the Middle East. There was no particular religious element involved in policy positions except as it involved the Israelis. For the Muslim masses and intellectuals, each case needs to be viewed separately. The ostracism of Egypt after Camp David saw mixed reactions arising from the need to balance antagonism toward Israel and the desire for Arab unity. Indonesian and Singaporean Muslim elites were probably less bothered by the first factor than those in Malaysia. Religion played a relatively small role in attitudes toward the Iran-Iraq War, with the probable exception of strong supporters of Iran's Islamic Revolution. For many Muslims, the balance of Israel, Arab unity, and fears of Western control of the Muslim people probably tilted because of greater weight given the fear of Western power. The fact that Israel did not enter the conflict surely lessened the level of Islamic antagonism toward the final defeat of Iraq.

MIDDLE EASTERN INVOLVEMENT IN SOUTHEAST ASIA

As noted in chapter 1, there was almost no Middle Eastern involvement or interest in Southeast Asian domestic and international issues before World War II. Poor communications and Southeast Asia's dependent status were both obstacles to knowledge and action. In the

early postwar years there was some interest in Indonesia's fight for
independence against the Dutch, although this was not usually expressed in religious terms. During the so-called confrontation between Malaysia and Indonesia in the early 1960s, there were also calls
for peace between the two Muslim nations. For example, the General
Islamic Conference meeting in Mecca in 1965 expressed deep regret at
this dispute between "Muslim brothers," stating that it could only aid
Islam's enemies.[38] However, in the postwar era, Middle Eastern concern with Southeast Asia has centered upon two areas, Muslim minorities and efforts to propagate particular interpretations of Islam.

The three Muslim minorities in Southeast Asia that have attracted
the attention of Muslims elsewhere are those in Burma, Thailand, and
the Philippines, with the last being the most prominent by far. The
Arakanese in Burma, a sizable portion of whom are Muslims, have
been involved in attempts to achieve greater autonomy or independence since the 1950s. Some unofficial aid was also received from
Pakistan and later Bangladesh, which also provided sanctuary for the
Arakanese.[39] Intermittent rebellion took place over many years, under the leadership of the Arakan Rohingya Islamic Front, which
sought support from the OIC and sent representatives to that organization.[40] Basically, little came of either the rebellion or efforts to obtain
outside support from the Islamic world. Again, in 1992 the OIC became involved with the plight of the Arakanese, who accused the
Burmese government of mistreatment.

The Malay-Muslim separatist activities in southern Thailand have
been of a larger and more longstanding nature, but they have not
been center stage in world Islamic forums.[41] The Malay-Muslims are
primarily concentrated in the four southern provinces of Thailand.
Following the formal incorporation of this region into the Thai Buddhist kingdom at the beginning of this century, intermittent violent
and nonviolent opposition to Thai rule has been manifested. Until the
1960s tensions were enhanced by Thai neglect of the region's development, the absence of Malay-Muslim governmental officials, an increase in Thai Buddhist encroachment on southern Muslim land, and
demands for greater recognition of ethnic-religious identity. The vitality of the movement has varied over the years, and there is now less
involvement in violent tactics, although the desire for autonomy and
equal rights remains strong. The movement has not been aided by

divisions among the separatist organizations and the presence of a long-term communist insurgency in the area. The latter made the region of greater strategic importance to Malaysia and Thailand and increased official military activity.

The OIC and Islamic Conference of Foreign Ministers have endorsed the right of autonomy for the Malay-Muslims of southern Thailand, although they have not provided formal recognition. Libya has been the Middle Eastern state most directly involved. It has provided sanctuary to rebel leaders and a podium from which these spokesmen can plead their cause. The presence of some 13,000 Thai workers in Libya has included individuals from the south who have, at the least, found a sympathetic political and religious environment.[42] Thai official sources have privately accused the Libyans of aiding the rebels more materially, and in 1985 an unnamed Middle Eastern country was charged by Thai intelligence of training guerrilla units abroad and sending them back to fight in Thailand.[43] Up to now, there has been no proof of Libyan military involvement. Khadaffi's support of the Thai Malays can be seen as part of an effort to counter the influence of more conservative Middle Eastern countries in the region and to project his power overseas.

Other support has come from Saudi Arabia, either directly or indirectly. Over the past twenty years, there have been ten to thirty thousand workers from southern Thailand in Saudi Arabia, and they have been an important source of funding to the secessionists. One of the major Malay-Muslim groups has an office in Mecca, supported by their countrymen in Saudi Arabia. Malay-Muslim organizations in southern Thailand have reportedly received funds from the Department of Scholarly Research and Religious Ruling of Saudi Arabia, the Islamic Development Bank, and Islamic Call of Kuwait.[44] There have also been reports of guerrilla training in Afghanistan, Syria, and Libya.

The most publicized Middle Eastern role in Southeast Asia has related to the so-called Moro issue in the southern Philippines.[45] The historic foundations of this conflict are analogous to the Thai case. Decades of neglect, the intrusion of non-Muslim people into traditional Islamic regions, the perception of domination by a *kafir* (infidel) government, and the increase in ethnic-religious identity worldwide have all exacerbated tensions. As in Thailand, there has been intermittent violent and nonviolent opposition to the central government throughout the century. During the postindependence era, armed opposition increased more than in Thailand. It is argued that during the 1970s at least 50,000 persons died in the fighting in the region. The largest insurgent group, the Moro National Liberation Front (MNLF) was able to mobilize some thirty thousand men in the early 1970s. However, the Moros have also been plagued by factionalism, and it has complicated international Islamic efforts to ameliorate the conflict. While the Moro insurgency continues in the southern Philippines, it appears that it had lost some of its vitality after President Corazon Aquino attained power.

When assessing what role outside Muslim groups play in the Moro problem, it is useful to divide the analysis between the actions of international organizations and the specific policies of Libya. From the early 1970s the international Islamic community has stated its formal support for much of the Moro position. In 1972 the ambassadors of Muslim countries with delegations in Manila held an inspection tour of the south, followed by other missions in the succeeding year. This was part of Marcos's strategy of attempting to show that the Moro issue was not simply a Muslim problem. The fifth Islamic Conference of Foreign Ministers held in Kuala Lumpur in 1974 called on the Philippines to "desist from all measures which resulted in the killing of Moslems," to halt military operations against the rebellion, and to negotiate with the Muslims.[46] However, the conference did not support secession.

In 1976 the conference secured the Tripoli Agreement, which was supposed to supply the basis for peace in the region. In succeeding years, the Islamic foreign ministers have continued their support of the Moros while at the same time refraining from either associating themselves with secessionist sentiment or demanding the use of economic sanctions against Manila. Conference members have also become involved in the internal conflicts within the Moro movement, tending to support the MNLF against other Muslim rivals. During this period, Muslim representatives at other meetings have lent their weight to the Moro movement, not always reflecting the somewhat more moderate stance of the foreign ministers. Manila was deeply worried when in the late 1980s the MNLF asked the OIC to become a full member of that organization. If the OIC agreed, it could have meant that, in accordance with its view of the PLO position, it might also agree to a separate Moro state. Malaysia and Indonesia played moderating roles during this period, working to keep the Philippines from being isolated from the rest of the world community. More important, both states wanted to keep ASEAN intact, the association to which all three states belonged. According to the Malaysian deputy prime minister at the time, Musa Hitam, ASEAN was paramount in Kuala Lumpur's concerns and the OIC was secondary.[47]

The importance of oil to the Philippines, combined with the financial impact of the large number of Filipino workers in the Middle East, has been a major factor in Manila's willingness to express at least oral agreement with moderate international efforts at negotiation. As one observer noted, "With the politics of oil thrown into the cauldron, the national economy could face collapse."[48] Reports that major oil exporters such as Saudi Arabia have been unhappy with the implementation of the Tripoli Agreement can only be further impetus to Manila's efforts to solve the problem.[49] At the same time, neither the Marcos nor the Aquino regime were able to achieve a peaceful solution and the rebellion continues.

The single most active Middle Eastern participant in the Moro conflict has been Libya. The Khadaffi government has varied its statements from conciliation to declarations such as "the misery faced by the Moslems in the southern Philippines is no less horrifying than that faced by the Palestinians."[50] Before the negotiation of the Tripoli Agreement between Khadaffi and Imelda Marcos, the former called for jihad and economic boycotts against Manila. In earlier years, Libya had also been responsible for sending arms and other aid to the insurgents and providing asylum to its members. There were reports that this material was transported through Sabah into Mindanao. However, in later years there were more friendly exchanges between the two governments and a major decline in material support of the rebellion by Libya.

It is far more difficult to analyze reports of possibly illicit clandestine Middle Eastern efforts to influence Southeast Asian domestic politics. It is not easy to verify government reports of foreign intervention, particularly when diplomacy often demands that charges be veiled and when evidence is often unavailable. Newspapers may mention an "unnamed Middle Eastern government," with leaks that

Iran or Libya are the real subjects. In chapter 4, the activities of Iran in Southeast Asia after the Iranian Revolution are assessed. The other country open to suspicion has been Libya. Over the past two decades there have been accusations of Libyan interference in Indonesian politics in support of Muslim radical groups in Java and Sumatra. Libya has also been questioned about aid to insurgents in southern Thailand and deviant elements in Malaysia. Unlike the Moro issue, Libya has not publicly declared its involvement in these cases. There has been no public outcry against interference by any other Middle Eastern country.

INTERNATIONAL ISLAMIC ORGANIZATIONS

In chapter 1 the prewar interest of many Southeast Asian Muslims with Pan-Islam and the caliphate movement was discussed. The post-independence period has seen the development of a range of Islamic organizations that have attracted the interest of people in the region. Before 1949, efforts at Pan-Islam were led by the Rabitat al alam al Islami based in Mecca, the International Islamic Organization headquartered in Jakarta, the World Moslem Conference in Karachi, and the Muktamar Islamy in Cairo.[51]

Following that era, the major groups have included nongovernmental associations such as the Muslim World Congress, founded in 1950, and the Muslim World League, established in 1962.[52] The former's principles call for the propagation of Islam and support of Muslim wars of liberation. It has received considerable Saudi money and has been active in publishing programs. The Muslim World League has been based in Mecca and has also been heavily funded by the Saudis. It has offices throughout the world and publishes journals in both Arabic and English. Like the World Congress, it advocates propagating Islam and confronting its enemies. The league has been active in coordinating the work of many other Islamic associations. In 1981 it implemented a training program for mosque leaders in Indonesia. Other nongovernmental organizations have included the World Association of Muslim Youth (WAMY), the Islamic Chamber of Commerce, the Supreme Word Council for Mosques (also supported by the Saudis), and a wide range of special issue groups and seminars. In 1982 the league gave half its annual budget of US$29 million for the maintenance of mosques in Southeast Asia.[53]

The most important government body has been the OIC, initiated by Muslim heads of state at Rabat, Morocco, in 1969. It is composed of some forty-five states and its formal objectives have been to increase Islamic solidarity, protect the holy places, support the people of Palestine, and strengthen the independence and national rights of Muslim peoples. To these ends, it has coordinated political stands on a variety of issues, the Palestine question particularly but also the Soviet occupation of Afghanistan, the Moro problem, and intra-Muslim conflicts. The OIC has developed cooperation in economic matters, including providing aid for the formation of the Islamic Development Bank, sponsoring discussions of a common market, and securing agreements on commercial and economic cooperation and technical development. Affiliated with the OIC is the Islamic Chambers of Commerce, Industry and Commodity Exchange. Finally, the OIC has actively helped to develop Islamic culture and education, forming an Islamic Economic and Social Council (ISESCO), reminiscent of UNESCO, and establishing an Islamic news agency and publishing program. It has frequently supplied funds for Islamic studies in Southeast Asia. Some critics of the OIC have questioned whether the large funds expended and political rhetoric of its meetings have had the impact they should have over its more than twenty years of activity.[54] Others have seen the OIC and other associations as vehicles for efforts of the government of Saudi Arabia to propagate and protect its own interpretation of Islam and Saudi political and economic interests.

Organizationally, the OIC is composed of the Conference of Kings and heads of state and governments, its supreme ruling body; the Conference of Foreign Ministers, which meets once a year or when needed; and the General Secretariat, which carries out the general administration of the organization. The first secretary-general of the Secretariat was Malaysia's first prime minister, Tengku Abdul Rahman.

As might be expected, the secular leadership of Indonesia has been somewhat less supportive of such organizations than Malaysia, although then President Sukarno did lend his aid for an Africa-Asia Islamic Conference in 1964. However, this was during the confrontation between Indonesia and Malaysia when both governments were attempting to gain support for their positions from groups outside the region. Given internal divisions in Indonesia and Jakarta's alienation from the United Nations at the time, greater attention was made to isolate Malaysia through nonaligned organizations. All Jakarta had received from the Security Council was a mild Norwegian-formulated resolution calling on all parties "to refrain from all threats or use of force and to respect the territorial integrity and political independence of each other."[55] Indonesia later felt humiliated by the election of Malaysia to the Security Council in 1965. Kuala Lumpur was more involved than Indonesia in seeking support from coreligionists both multilaterally and through bilateral diplomacy. To counter this, Indonesia also sought allies from the Muslim world but was not particularly successful.

During the Suharto era, Indonesia, although again supportive of the United Nations and somewhat less involved in nonaligned politics, did not seek to identify itself closely with organizations such as the OIC. It did not participate formally in the Rabat and Jeddah conferences of 1969 and 1970 that formed the OIC. Indonesia did attend the 1972 meeting that promulgated the charter of the Islamic Conference but did not become a signatory to it. Indonesian leaders reasoned that if Indonesia became a full member and signatory it would have to accept the OIC's Muslim principles and formally declare itself an Islamic state. The care with which the Indonesian government has confronted this issue can be seen by Foreign Minister Mochtar Kusumaatmadja's statement that "without in any way diminishing the meaning and importance of Panchasila as the philosophical basis of the nation, Indonesian membership in the ICO [OIC] is an indication that our foreign policy cannot ignore the reality that 88 percent of our population belongs to the Muslim religion."[56] Jakarta's view of the OIC was probably best summed up by a Foreign Ministry official who declared, "We don't want to have an Islamic orientation in our foreign policy for reasons of domestic politics, among others. I don't mean to imply that the Muslims are not loyal, but . . . if the domestic situation continues to stabilize in an overall sense, perhaps then we will feel that the ICO [OIC] is a more useful vehicle for advancing our interests. But what would we gain by joining formally and fully? After all, for all practical purposes it doesn't really matter whether or not Indonesia is a signatory of the Islamic Charter. It's a non-issue."[57]

In the ensuing years, Jakarta has become more closely identified with the OIC and has entered into discussions over such issues as the

Moro problem and ostracism of Egypt after Camp David. It also signed the General Agreement on Economic, Technical, and Commercial Cooperation among Member Countries of the Islamic Conference and hosted the OIC's Islamic Chamber of Commerce in 1983. Indonesia has always been represented in the Secretariat of Islamic Countries and Islamic Development Bank. There has also been public and private support for the activities of nongovernmental international Islamic organizations. For example, President Suharto opened the first World Islamic Mass Media Conference, which has ties to the World Islamic League.[58] M. Natsir has been vice-president of Rabitat al alam al Islami, an international religious organization; an Indonesian has been secretary-general of the Islamic International Federation of Student Organizations; and from 1972 to 1975 an Indonesian was one of the secretaries of WAMY.[59]

Malaysia, for its part, has been committed to fostering close relations with a plethora of Muslim organizations. Tengku Abdul Rahman, while still prime minister, made an abortive attempt in 1961 and 1962 to promulgate a Muslim Commonwealth patterned after the British one.[60] Since that period Malaysia has hosted, been a member of, or had major offices in numerous Muslim groups. For example, it hosted the fourteen-state Islamic Conference in 1969, the first meeting of the Governors of Central Banks of the OIC in 1978, the second annual meeting of the Board of Governors of the Islamic Development Bank in the same year, the Council of Foreign Ministers of the OIC more than once, and many regional Islamic symposia and seminars. Some have even complained that too many Islamic conferences were being hosted in Malaysia. As noted previously, Tengku was also the OIC's first secretary-general and Anwar Ibrahim, when he was president of the youth group ABIM, was elected more than once as head of WAMY for Asia and the Pacific.

At the venues of these conferences, Malaysia sought to play a leading role in formulating and implementing policy. It supported OIC positions vis-à-vis Israel, Soviet actions in Afghanistan, and a wide range of economic and cultural resolutions. Malaysian prime ministers and foreign ministers made it a point to attend these meetings, and their remarks were fully covered in the local media. Internationally, this gave the small nation a prominent role. Domestically, it provided the government with an aura of legitimacy as the protector of Islam, a position that aided it in gathering support from its Malay-Muslim constituency.

CONCLUSION

Three points can be made in summation. First, it is obvious that the postwar years have seen a major increase in political interaction between the Middle East and Southeast Asia. Middle Eastern states have become involved in Southeast Asian affairs, either bilaterally or through international Islamic institutions. This involvement has been publicly implemented with regard to Muslim minorities in Thailand, Burma, and the Philippines and may have taken place clandestinely by states such as Iran and Libya in support of opposition domestic Muslim groups. Southeast Asian states have expressed their views and from time to time engaged in diplomatic efforts with regard to Middle Eastern disputes, from the Arab-Israeli conflict to the Soviet invasion of Afghanistan. Further, a wide range of international Islamic institutions has developed that have increasingly involved Southeast Asian countries and issues. This increase in interaction can be traced in part to the postwar independence movements that formed sovereign states capable of formulating their own foreign policies and partly to an increased awareness of Islamic and Third World solidarity.

Second, Islam is a major factor in explaining the type of political interaction implemented by individual Southeast Asian states. Non-Muslim governments with Muslim minorities have recognized the importance of maintaining good relations with Middle Eastern countries. This stance has resulted from the combination of the need to defend important economic interests derived from oil imports, receipt of funds from workers in the Middle East, the hope for Arab investments, and increased Arab interest in the problems of these minorities. As we have seen, the effort by Marcos to expand Philippine relations with Muslim states in the early 1970s was a direct result of these factors.

For Indonesia and Malaysia, Islamic domestic politics have framed their attitudes toward relations with the Middle East. Jakarta's worries over the challenge of elements of its Muslim population have been an important factor in its playing down of Islam as the grounds for its foreign policy decisions and in its emphasis on Third World aims. Malaysia's postindependence government, on the other hand, has concluded that the best means of meeting the challenge of its Muslim opposition has been to stress its worldwide Islamic ties and thus underscore its religious legitimacy. Also, as a small country it has been able to play a greater international role than would otherwise be expected by actively engaging in world Islamic politics.

Finally, notwithstanding the aforementioned developments, these regions remain concentrated upon political problems in their own areas, and both Islamic international organizations and activities in the other region are secondary. The Middle East has been beset with a multitude of postwar conflicts, and the participation or support of Southeast Asian states has been perceived to be of peripheral importance at best. To most of the Southeast Asian countries, regional issues and the maintenance of ASEAN have been far more central than what has taken place in the Middle East. The one exception would be the Israeli problem, which can inflame emotions among Muslims throughout the world. As for Middle Eastern involvement in Southeast Asia, it has been barely tolerated with regard to Muslim minority problems and actively opposed when it has come to reported interference in Indonesia's and Malaysia's domestic affairs.

Chapter 4

THE IRANIAN CONNECTION

 The amount of conjecture, accusation, and emotional reporting that has accompanied journalistic interpretations and governmental statements regarding the entrance of the Iranian Revolution into Southeast Asia demands a separate assessment of this phenomenon. Again, the emphasis will be on Indonesia and Malaysia, given the greater alleged impact of the Revolution in those countries. This chapter is focused on three areas: official relations between Iran and selected governments in Southeast Asia; efforts by local authorities to contain the influence of the Revolution on their people; and popular attitudes toward the Revolution.

STATE-TO-STATE RELATIONS

If the uninformed observer simply read the official statements of Iranian and Southeast Asian officials and noted the comings and goings of diplomats and political leaders, it would appear that little was changed by the Iranian Islamic Revolution. However, this external normalcy hid serious worries among Southeast Asian authorities about the effects of events in Iran on their citizens. Nevertheless, neither Jakarta nor Kuala Lumpur particularly wished to be seen publicly criticizing a seeming victory of Islam over Western imperialism and secular behavior. Similarly, states with Muslim minorities did not want to exacerbate local tensions further or possibly invite outside intervention.

Initially, the official reaction to the overthrow of the shah in 1979 was silence: no favorable, unfavorable, or neutral statement emanated from either the Indonesian or Malaysian regime. It was not until later in the year that the Malaysian foreign minister, in answer to a question in the Malayan parliament, the Dewan Rakyat, stated that relations between Iran and Malaysia were "normal" and that the formation of the revolutionary government in Iran was part of "the internal affairs of Iran." He also noted that diplomatic personnel were carrying out their duties as usual.[1]

The Indonesian government was even more reticent, carefully avoiding comment on the ousting of the shah and on the efforts to release the American hostages. Nor was President Suharto willing to act as a mediator in these affairs. As Sharon Siddique wrote, the hostage question was not an easy issue for either country: "In Indonesia and Malaysia particularly, this official silence reflects the dilemma of being caught between the pragmatic considerations of the government's support for the principles of international law and the emotional identification on the part of many Indonesian and Malaysian citizens with the idea of a just and egalitarian state in Iran."[2] Even during the long Iran-Iraq War, when the Malaysians were prepared to help mediate the conflict and participated in the OIC Peace Committee, the Indonesian government remained largely silent. Ultimately, the most either country actually did was decry bloodshed between fellow believers, and Jakarta and Kuala Lumpur maintained a neutral stance toward the combatants.

It can be argued that in the period immediately following the fall of the shah there were other equally or more important issues that confronted both governments and held the attention of the press. These included the plight of the great numbers of Vietnamese "boat people" landing on their shores, President Carter's Middle East peace talks, a major row over a Malaysian airline strike, and Chinese attacks on the northern border of Vietnam. Yet these events do not fully explain the official silence. As we shall see, the explanation appears to lie in the domestic problems raised by the Iranian Revolution.

Formal diplomatic relations, including the establishment of embassies in Tehran and Southeast Asian capitals had already taken place between Iran and several countries in the region (including Indonesia, Thailand, and Malaysia), although ambassadors were not always named.[3] In the first decade after the fall of the shah, however, there was a continued and even expanded pattern of official visits, particularly of Iranian officials to Southeast Asia. A list of comings and goings illustrates this interaction.

1980   Iranian industrial minister to Malaysia.
1981   Iranian speaker Hashemi Rafsanjani visits Kuala Lumpur and meets Mahathir.
1982   Iran establishes an embassy in Kuala Lumpur; Khoumeini receives outgoing Indonesian envoy.
1983   Iranian Foreign Ministry official meets with Indonesian counterparts.
1984   Iranian foreign minister goes to Malaysia; Indonesian commercial delegation visits Iran; Malaysian foreign minister visits Iran.
1985   Khoumeini receives Malaysian envoy.
1986   Suharto meets with Iranians to discuss expansion of relations. Iranian foreign minister receives first Malaysian envoy.
1987   Indonesian foreign minister visits Iran.
1988   Rafsanjani again to Malaysia; Malaysian foreign minister visits Tehran; Khoumeini receives outgoing Indonesian envoy.

Thus, all appeared well, at least on the surface. But if diplomatic relations continued in the "normal" pattern, the Revolution and subsequent Iran-Iraq War severely limited trade and investment opportunities between Iran and Southeast Asia. As noted in chapter 2, important economic relations had begun between the two regions, and Iran had started to invest in Southeast Asia, particularly in the Philippines. However, while other Middle Eastern states were increasing their economic ties with Southeast Asia, Iranian trade remained the lowest of the major Middle Eastern countries. The relatively small Indonesian and Malaysian work forces that were in Iran in 1978–79 had all but disappeared by 1980, and Iranian investments in Southeast Asia were virtually nonexistent.[4]

Trade did not collapse between Iran and Southeast Asia, but when contrasted with other Middle Eastern states it was obvious that domestic and international conditions facing Iran had an adverse effect. By the end of the 1980s, Iranian trade with Indonesia was below its trade with Saudi Arabia, Kuwait, Yemen, Bahrain, Libya, Jordan, the UAE, Morocco, and Egypt. With Malaysia, it was below trade with Egypt, Saudi Arabia, Kuwait, Jordan, the Yemens, and Iraq.[5]

One striking aspect of Iranian trade at that time was the generally favorable balance with Southeast Asian states. In 1987 Malaysia, for example, had a negative balance of trade with major oil exporters such as Saudi Arabia and Kuwait, while it had a favorable balance with Iran of 10 to 1. For Thailand, which had a favorable balance of trade of about 3 to 1 in 1980, the ratio hit approximately 9 to 1 by 1984.[6] It was only after the end of the Iran-Iraq conflict that serious efforts began to restore trade ties. In sum, during much of the 1980s state-to-state relations were generally quiet politically and stagnant economically.

GOVERNMENT ATTITUDES TOWARD THE REVOLUTION

While official relations continued at a seemingly tranquil pace, the actions taken by Jakarta, Kuala Lumpur, Manila, and Bangkok to control any unfavorable local impact of the revolution demonstrated the concerns the authorities had about events in Iran. These concerns relate to domestic policy issues delineated in chapter 3. Any analysis of Southeast Asian governments' efforts to deal with the impact of events in Iran is plagued by severe limitations. First, these regimes have not publicly and completely delineated their policies in detail, as they have been caught in the dilemma of wishing to control undesirable behavior while not openly attacking a movement with strong religious and emotional ties. Second, although there have been numerous charges of possible Middle Eastern interference in Southeast Asian Islamic affairs, there is little concrete evidence. Third, not all deviant interpretations of Islam originate in Iran or are considered by the respective governments as Iranian-inspired. Thus, when accusations have been made, it has not always been easy to identify the instigator, which is frequently not Iran.

Throughout Southeast Asia in the 1980s there were hints of Iranian efforts to gain support for the Revolution from the local Muslim community or even that Tehran was active in fomenting antigovernment activities. Various press reports, denied by the Iranian Embassy, indicate that the Iranian government has been warned by the Malaysian authorities against interfering in domestic matters. In 1979 the press published veiled statements from both the deputy prime minister and the inspector general of police that certain religious groups were seeking to overthrow the government.[7] In 1982 a Penang newspaper, the *Star*, reported that the Iranian Embassy had been told to curtail certain links with groups working to set up an Islamic state.[8] These groups allegedly included Malaysians arrested in Saudi Arabia during the haj season for passing out anti-Saudi, pro-Iranian material that had been sponsored by "an Islamic country"; seditious groups and individuals, including several government figures and top officials of "a certain bank," who desired an Islamic state; and visitors seeking to teach and promote the advantages of an Islamic government.

A later article in the *New Straits Times*, often an outlet of official policy, stated that the Malaysian home minister had sought to regulate traffic of allegedly revolutionary individuals between Iran and Malaysia.[9] In the aforementioned case, Deputy Prime Minister Musa Hitam had accused unnamed political groups of plotting a revolution to make Malaysia an Islamic republic. An unidentified Islamic country, apparently Iran, was supposedly aiding these elements. At a later meeting with a high-level Iranian trade delegation, Musa reportedly expressed concern over "any misinterpretation and application of the Iranian experience and situation" in Malaysia.[10] There were also frequent accusations that the main nongovernmental dakwah organization, ABIM, a group then perceived as a threat to the government, had links with Iran.[11] The visit of its leader to Tehran soon after the Revolution did little to diminish that fear.

In Indonesia there have been allegations, but no firm evidence, of the existence of seditious groups seeking support from Iran or Libya. Examples abound. An organization called the Indonesian Islamic Revolution Board was accused of seeking Iranian support to overthrow the Suharto regime. In the 1986 prosecution of those accused of the Malang bombings there were allegations of a Shi'i network centering on two Muslim preachers. One allegedly fled to Iran where he had apparently been a student in 1982–84.[12]

There have also been charges that Muslim radicals have sought to implement an Islamic state in the pattern of Iran. In one well-publicized case, Irfan Suryahadi, editor of the Indonesian Muslim youth magazine *Al Risalah*, was sentenced to thirteen years' imprisonment for subversion. Among the articles in the magazine that were used against him was one entitled "The Advice of Ayatollah Khoumeini" (*Wejangan Ayatullah Khoumeini*). Prosecutors alleged that this piece incited a "stirring-up of Islamic Revolution to destroy governments not based upon Islam and to invite Muslims throughout the world to bring Islamic revolution to fruition." Suryahadi was also reported to have admitted frequent contacts with the Iranian Embassy in Jakarta. While raiding his office, authorities claimed they confiscated the Iranian Embassy newsletter "Yaum al Quds." They asserted that *Al Risalah* was funded by the Middle East and called upon the Iranian Embassy to send copies of its newsletter to the Indonesian government prior to local distribution (somewhat similar controls have been established in Malaysia).[13] But it would be incorrect to state that the Indonesian authorities underscored the Iranian connection in the series of antisedition trials that charged Islamic "radicals" with attempts to overthrow the regime or speak against its policies (particularly the Panchasila). A review of the charges and defense of religious defendants during 1985 and 1986 uncovers little reference to the Iranian Revolution or Iranian influence.

The Iranian Revolution has also spilled over into other Southeast Asian states. In the Philippines there were economic as well as political consequences to the fall of the shah.[14] The shah had held property, bank deposits, and stock shares in land corporations and had some student support from one section of the some 2,500 to 3,500 Iranian students studying in the Philippines. These students and supporters of the Revolution fought pitched battles in Manila in the early 1980s. At one time, about 300 people shouting "Death to Khoumeini" clashed with pro-Khoumeini groups, and many were arrested.[15] These clashes continued into 1982.[16] However, the most vocal Iranian voices in the Philippines came from prorevolution students who actively supported Khoumeini during this period.[17] There were also numerous although unproven reports of "killer squads" charged with eliminating pro-shah and anti-Khoumeini Iranian students. The Filipino press expressed considerable concern over student activities, and there were calls for deportation of troublemakers. The Philippine government was also worried and attempted to control Iranian enrollment in the country's universities.

Manila was displeased, too, with Iran's vocal support of the Moro secessionist movement. MNLF leaders visited Tehran soon after the Revolution and over time met with almost all the major leaders of the Revolution. The MNLF received official recognition by the Iranian government in November 1980 and was treated as an embassy with regard to formal functions. There have been regular reports of economic aid to the secessionists, although there is no direct evidence of it. However, in 1979 the Iranian oil minister accused Manila of a massacre of the Moros and suspended oil exports to the Philippines. He stated that Iran would not supply "a single drop of oil as long as oppression and massacre of Muslims continue there."[18] MNLF spokesmen attempted to use the Iranian embargo to get other Middle Eastern countries to follow Tehran's lead but were not successful.

In the early 1980s Manila was also concerned that the literature from the Revolution might influence its Muslim population. The availability of such material increased and governmental fears were not lessened by statements from local Iranian students such as "These we have distributed among our Filipino brothers in this country and we say we have awakened them from their slumber. We have succeeded in enlightening and effectively provoking the Filipino masses— Muslims and Christians alike—to take overt actions against the corrupt regime of prostitutes and dictator. . . . They have learned what we have taught them in the art and science of revolution and can proudly say now that they have their underground movements patterned after the one we started in Iran."[19]

In Bangkok, Thailand, there has long been an intellectual interest in Shi'ism. As noted in chapter 3, the Malay-Muslim provinces of southern Thailand have long been centers of separatist religious-ethnic sentiment. There were no signs of significant Shi'i influence there until mid-1990, when this pattern appeared to change.

In 1989 and 1990 four Saudi diplomats were murdered after Saudi warnings of an assassination campaign, allegedly aided by the Iranians. There is no public evidence to tie Iran to the killings, but the Saudis were sufficiently aggravated to stop providing visas to Thai workers.[20] There were rumors that Iran was providing military training to Thai separatists, a point denied by the Iranian ambassador in late June 1990. He stated that separatism was a Thai domestic problem.[21] Earlier that month some ten to twenty thousand Muslims gathered at a rally at the Kruze mosque in Pattani.[22] The two chief organizers of the rally, Sorayuth Sakulnasantisart and Pairote Sasanaphibaan, had allegedly been influenced by Shi'i ideas from Iran. The gathering was told "to be prepared to die for their Islamic cause" should there be violence by Thai security forces. It has been argued that the majority of those attending were not aware that the gathering would be political, and apparently there were no Shiʻi teachings by the speakers. There were alleged calls for armed rebellion against the Thai state and references for support from an unknown Middle Eastern country. Military authorities believe that there are only one hundred Shiʻi converts in the southern region, and there is no evidence of relationships with other militant separatists.

The Malaysian and Indonesian governments have been the most active in attempting to limit undesirable interaction with Iran. They have discouraged both private visits to Iran and students going to Iran for religious studies. This policy was unofficial in the first years after the Revolution, and those citizens returning from Iran were reportedly held in suspicion by authorities. However, in the mid-1980s the Indonesian government formally barred its citizens from studying in thirty-one countries. Of those states, twenty-one were communist, four were those with which Indonesia had no diplomatic relations for politically sensitive reasons (Israel, South Africa, Taiwan, and Portugal), and six were Muslim countries defined as "extreme" (Libya, Iran, Iraq, Syria, Lebanon, and Algeria).[23]

There have also been veiled and not-so-veiled warnings from the governments against deviant behavior and ideas, which would appear to include the ideology of the Iranian Revolution. These statements have ranged from relatively neutral ones (such as Prime Minister Mahathir's comments that one Islamic country could not be compared with another and that the glory of Islam could not be achieved with slogans)[24] to more direct analyses (characterized by the previously noted statement of Musa Hitam and by the view of Religious Affairs Minister Haji Munawir Sjadzali that "although the extremist movement became stronger since the Islamic Revolution in 1979, the Muslims generally do not favor the militant approach")[25] and finally to blatant charges that deviant religious ideas seek to destroy "true Islam." While not expecting either state to become "another Iran," both governments have seen danger in ideas that might lend support to their radical opposition or that might reinforce the beliefs of mainstream Muslims to the point where inter- or intrareligious friction might be exacerbated. In addition, cynics argue that by playing up the extremists and publicizing their statements and rare acts of violence, the authorities will frighten other Muslims away from possible subversive religious ideas; by branding less radical opponents as tied to these deviants, then, the governments can weaken popular support for the opposition.

Thus, one of the most important effects of the Iranian Revolution on the governments of Malaysia and Indonesia was to increase their efforts to control the political role of those Islamic forces seen as detrimental to state policies. Partly because of events in Iran, both Jakarta and Kuala Lumpur became increasingly aware of the dangers posed by religious ideology. They sought to contain the negative aspects through a combination of cooptation, threats, increased religious observance and rhetoric, and greater surveillance of religious activists.[26]

POPULAR ATTITUDES TOWARD THE REVOLUTION

This history of governments' attitudes toward the Iranian Revolution brings us to the core questions regarding the impact of the Revolution on Southeast Asia. How much has the Iranian experience actually penetrated the thinking of the populace? Have the fears of the authorities been justified? How accurate were some of the early pundits who predicted that countries like Malaysia and Indonesia would become another Iran? To answer these questions, it is important to consider several key factors. These include the viability of Shi'i communities in the region that would supposedly be more vulnerable than the Sunni population to the principles espoused by the Revolution; the impact of revolutionary and prerevolutionary religious thinking on the majority Muslim population of Southeast Asia; and the degree to which these attitudes may have changed over time. Again, methodological barriers block a complete understanding of these issues. Given the antagonistic views of the governments involved to the Revolution and its philosophy, as well as the absence of politically sensitive polling, it is difficult to gauge public attitudes accurately. This difficulty does not prevent the observer from observing major trends. Nor can it be argued that the absence of sizable pro-Iranian organizations and the lack of a similar uprising in Malaysia and Indonesia are simply the result of government repression.

Although we will return to the intellectual impact of Shi'i thought in the next chapter, it is important to note here that there is no large Shi'i community in Southeast Asia. Most Muslims who immigrated to Southeast Asia came from Arabia or the Indian subcontinent and were Sunni. There is evidence of early Shi'i influence in Southeast Asia, but none of the elements of that period impacted on contemporary Shi'i thought in the region.[27] Earlier the small but growing Shi'i group in southern Thailand and the Iranian student population in the Philippines was discussed. There is also some Shi'i influence on intellectual Muslim interpretations in Indonesia. However, there is no major Shi'i community in Southeast Asia and thus no natural base for Iranian influence as exists in parts of the Middle East.

What then of the Sunni majority? To judge the impact of the Iranian Revolution on the Sunni-dominated communities, we look at three major indicators: the literature on or by Khoumeini and other Iranian religious thinkers available in Southeast Asia; references to the Revolution in the press and Islamic journals of the region; and reactions by Islamic organizations and activists. This type of evidence is tainted by government efforts to limit the effects of the Revolution, which may lead to understating the actual influence of the Iranian experience.

There have been many translations of Muslim activists in Southeast Asia and interpretive articles analyzing their theological and political views, but relatively few such works deal directly with the premier figure of the Iranian Revolution, Ayatollah Khoumeini. This does not mean that there were not articles describing the Revolution and Khoumeini's role, but I am talking about analytical pieces on his philosophy and goals. The relative shortage of these writings may be partly due to fear of government reprisals. However, it may be that Khoumeini's writings and statements have been primarily Iranian in character and therefore of limited attraction to scholars and activists in Southeast Asia. In particular, the role of the clergy, particularly Shi'i elements of his statements, and calls for strict adherence to Islamic law have not found ready adherents among younger and more modern Muslims.

Although Khoumeini's ideas may have been carefully monitored and contained by authorities, there has been a ready market in Indonesia and Malaysia for the writings of men who were influential in developing the ideology of the Iranian Revolution. In 1982 a publishing house called Nizan, which published Shi'i books, was established in Bandung, Indonesia.[28] Perhaps the best example of a popular pre-cursor of Khoumeini is the works of Ali Shariati, a key intellectual forerunner of the changes that rocked Iran after 1979.

Shariati has been credited with going beyond the narrow confines of Arab-based, more secular interpretations of Islam (such as Arab socialism) to provide a more universal religious ideology founded on Islam itself.[29] It can be argued that his views were broader and more universally attractive than those expressed by contemporary leaders of the revolution. Certainly Shariati, along with Qutb, Maududi, Al-Banna, and others, has been published widely in both Indonesia and Malaysia. During the 1980s, translations of many of Shariati's books and tracts have appeared in Indonesia: *Holy Book* (1982), *Haji* (1983), *Islamic Criticism of Marxism and Other Western Fallacies* (1983), *Islam in the Perspective of Religious Sociology* (1983), *Ideological Intellectuals* (1985), *The Role of the Intellectual Muslim* (1985), *Nobility* (1987), and *Once More* (1987). There have also been articles by or about Shariati in such journals as *Al-Nahdah, Prisma,* and *Dakwah.*

In some instances, Shariati's Iranian roots and relationship to the Revolution are clearly noted, while in others he is defined as a con-temporary revivalist or radical religious commentator. What appeared to resonate the most among Indonesian youth were his attacks upon rich Muslim oppressors and support of equity in society. In an Indo-nesia perceived by many young Muslims as controlled by imperialists in league with the military and corrupt businessmen, the writings of Shariati and the victory of Islam over the shah and his cohorts were attractive.

Analyses of the religious aspects of the Revolution itself have only appeared intermittently in the press and Muslim journals. However, during the first year after the fall of the shah, there was a deluge of articles in local-language publications discussing the events in Iran and the religious context of the rise of Khoumeini.[30] The English-language press displayed less interest: many articles simply detailed events with little comment. When they did analyze, Malaysian English-language papers were likely to underscore the instability sur-rounding the post-shah era. In general, the press was cautious about praising the policies of the Revolution itself or recommending those policies in Southeast Asia. Singaporean and Malaysian newspapers noted the difficulties of putting power in the hands of religious leadership, commenting on such issues as the role of women. There were also warnings of the propriety of Southeast Asians looking to a foreign leader.[31] However, published interviews with individuals returning from Iran explained what was taking place. They often applauded the victory of Islam in Iran but with the qualifier that as a model the Iranian Revolution was not applicable to Southeast Asia.

During the next decade, the patterns of reporting and religious analysis changed somewhat. A review of journal and newspaper articles shows a high percentage covered the Iran-Iraq War; their general perspective was that the conflict was disruptive of Islamic unity and could only aid its enemies.[32] The war, along with the character of the regime in Iran, incidents such as the rioting in Mecca, and the obvious governmental discouragement of prorevolutionary rhetoric and support, largely explains the diminishment in positive articles about what was taking place in Iran. Nonetheless, journal articles proclaiming the importance of the Revolution and some of its significant contributions to the people of Iran continued to appear. But the overall thrust of these articles became more objective critical analyses of the character of the Revolution as it played itself out in Iran.

We can also assess the impact of the Revolution through the reactions of Muslim organizations and activists. We have already noted the still somewhat isolated opposition movements in Thailand and the Philippines. From the beginning, there were demands from Islamic missionary and political organizations in Malaysia and Indonesia that their governments show more support for the Revolution. For example, the ABIM Federal Territory secretary asked the Malaysian government to support the struggles of Iranians to realize an Islamic republic.[33] When ABIM president Anwar Ibrahim (later successively minister of education, agriculture, and finance) returned from a meeting with Khoumeini in Iran, he joined with religious leaders from other countries in calling for an "Iranian Liberation/Solidarity Day" to be held on March 16, 1979. While noting that the Revolution was not a model for Malaysia, he stated, "We support the recent events in Iran because of the strength of Islam in opposing a cruel regime but we also support the Islamic movements in Pakistan and the Sudan who cooperate with the present leadership to determine peace and justice based on the principles of Islam."[34]

In 1982 the ABIM journal *Al-Risalah* praised certain accomplishments of the new regime, such as its ability to control drugs, alcohol, gambling, and prostitution.[35] Although more cautious in its support, the Malay-Muslim opposition party, PAS, was initially prepared to praise events in Iran. But PAS, like ABIM, was careful not to call for a similar revolution in Malaysia. Both ABIM and PAS have been accused by their political opponents of close links to Iran, but there is no evidence of formal ties.

As noted, in Indonesia there have been many government charges of radical Muslim groups supporting an "Iran-type" Islamic state or advocating the overthrow of the regime to further the Islamic cause. However, there is no proof that mainstream Islamic organizations went any farther than their Malaysian counterparts; that is, they may find satisfaction in the Islamic victory in Iran, but they do not encourage the model for Indonesia. In fact, a review of the many Islamic sermons and religious talks, several of which have been classified as subversive by the Indonesian government, reveals little mention of the Iranian Revolution or Khoumeini. When there are references to contemporary individuals, they are more likely to be local scholars or Middle Eastern writers of an earlier era.[36]

This paucity of subversive comment in sermons runs counter to the assumption that the infrequency of pro-Iranian oratory has simply been due to government censorship. Nor can it be argued that the educated Indonesian people know little about events in Iran. Both religious journals and news magazines have featured Khoumeini on their covers and followed early events in Iran regularly. One observer even commented that he thought that Khoumeini was the third most popular figure in Indonesia behind the current and former presidents of the republic. However, I believe that this interest in Khoumeini flourished because he symbolized the victory of Islam, not because Southeast Asians support the manner in which the Iranian Revolution developed.

Yet, based upon the comments of a wide range of observers of contemporary Islam in Southeast Asia, the general consensus is that the Iranian Revolution had an important influence on the religiously conscious elements in the region. It came at a time when the Islamic revival was gaining momentum in the area and Muslims, whether a majority or minority in their countries, were becoming more aware of their own identities. It was a period when the revivalist interpretations of Maududi, Qutb, and Shariati were beginning to make an impression on many activists. Locally, Muslims were increasing their contacts with Western materialism and morality and finding the meetings unsettling and often undesirable. It was also a time when Western ideological solutions put forward by the region's secular leaders were found wanting.[37] In this environment, the Iranian Revolution appeared at first to be an example of the victory of Islam over just those forces of Western imperialism, immorality, and ideology. That context is why the initial public reaction to the Iranian Revolution was generally so positive and why religious leaders were attracted to it. It was not necessarily a vote in favor of the specific institutional structures established in Iran or to the religious laws that were promulgated. To many Southeast Asians, it was the Revolution as symbol rather than reality that was so compelling.

The efforts of the Iranian Islamic community to overthrow the shah also found resonance in the view of many Southeast Asians of the need for struggle (*perjuangan ummat Islam*) to achieve an Islamic society. While this concept can mean many things—from the formation of an Islamic state to the greater implementation of Islamic principles— the very real, historic requirement of Southeast Asian Muslims to obtain their goals and make manifest the destiny of Islam gave added impetus to the support of the Revolution in Iran.[38]

Finally, as the Muslim intellectual Dawan Rahardjo observed, for many Indonesians there were important analogies between Iran and their country. These include Iran's efforts to free itself from a superpower, the employment of oil revenues for development, and the use of Islam to free Iran from capitalism and socialism at the national and international levels.[39]

However, some of the specific policies adopted by revolutionary Iran after 1979 were difficult for Southeast Asian Muslims to accept. Among the factors that had a generally negative impact were the increased role of the clergy in the Iranian government, the reports of harsh treatment of secular and religious opponents of the regime, the actions of Iranians abroad (such as the demonstrations in Mecca), the bloody Iran-Iraq conflict with the seeming intransigence of both sides, and the alleged state-supported attacks on other Muslims outside Iran. When these perceptions were combined with local government efforts to contain the influence of radical and deviant forces, the luster of Iran as a model diminished noticeably. But the initial phenomenon is still viewed by many as a major milestone on the road to the inevitable victory of Islam. In terms of its symbolic power, the success of the Iranian Revolution is analogous to the Japanese victory in the Russo-Japanese War, which was perceived by many Southeast Asian nationalists as the first real triumph of Asians over Europeans.

CONCLUSION

If we analyze the influence of the Iranian Revolution on Southeast Asia in terms of readily verifiable concrete evidence, we may miss the depth of the Revolution's impact. State-to-state relations have generally been proper, and the intergovernmental tensions that do exist have not broken out of polite diplomatic exchanges and veiled criticisms. At the same time, the Malaysian and Indonesian governments have fully recognized the threats to political and religious stability inherent in Iranian events. This recognition has led Jakarta and Kuala Lumpur to work to control Islamic ideas perceived to be subversive or detrimental to "peace and order." Such control was not a major problem for governments with Muslim minorities until the late 1980s, when the Revolution affected southern Thailand. Malaysia and Indonesia continued normal relations at the official level but made active efforts to ensure that the ideas of the Revolution did not penetrate local communities too deeply. Most threatening was that Iran would become a model for the establishment of new Islamic states in Southeast Asia.

It can be argued that the indigenous cultures and nature of Islam in the region are fundamentally antithetical to such a movement. Yet governments with both majority and minority Muslim communities have been faced with opponents deeply committed to fundamental religious changes. Admittedly, mainstream religious opposition has not publicly advocated the establishment of another Iran, although the formation of a state administered according to more structured Islamic legal and social principles has been espoused by some Muslim political organizations. However, to the degree that the Revolution touched emotional nerves of religious elements within the population, it gave warnings to the establishment that radical Islam needed to be carefully controlled.

Although some of the evidence is admittedly impressionistic, it appears that the Revolution itself had a major effect on religiously conscious elements in Southeast Asia. It fed into a series of other forces that were lending strength to the Islamic revival in the region. The perceived excesses of the new regime in Tehran and the long Iran-Iraq War weakened the original emotional attraction of many activists to the Iranian experience. Nevertheless, the Revolution is still viewed by a wide spectrum of Southeast Asian Muslims as one of the most important phenomena of the twentieth century. Nowhere else has Islam been so decidedly victorious over the economic, political, and moral forces of the West.

Many initially thought that Malaysia and Indonesia were possible candidates to be another Iran. Today it would be difficult to make that prognosis, at least for the foreseeable future. Not only have events in Iran made that less likely, but, more importantly, those in authority in Malaysia and Indonesia have, at least for the time being, weakened those elements in their countries seeking radical religious solutions. In Malaysia this has been accomplished through cooptation of many of the ideas and leaders of the religious opposition, combined with the threat and use of state power to limit the influence of those Muslim activists who propound what the government defines as radical or un-Islamic views. The Indonesian government initially was more prepared to use its power and authority to ensure that dissident religious groups and ideas did not gain preeminence, and, at least for now, the larger religious organizations have seen their political power seriously eroded. Where there are minority Muslim groups, they do not have the numbers or power to be able to establish any meaningful independent Muslim political order, whether Iranian-influenced or not. Beyond state policies, the religious cultures of Southeast Asia make questionable the successful transfer of the Iranian model to the region. The syncretic nature of Indonesian Islam and traditional loyalties of Malay systems are not fertile grounds for another Iran.

Chapter 5

INTELLECTUAL INTERACTION

 For those familiar with postwar Southeast Asia, one of the remarkable changes in the region has been the broadening of the horizons of intellectual life. An important aspect of this pattern has been the increased penetration of foreign ideas into the region. One has only to roam the bookstores of Singapore, Kuala Lumpur, or Jakarta to see the breadth of literature available to the populace or the expansion of secondary and university education in every country in the area. This is not to say that Southeast Asia was a vast intellectual wasteland before the war. It is only necessary to read Soetan Sjahrir's *Out of Exile*,[1] review the activities of the Marxist Study Club in Burma, or read the works of J. Rizal, the father of Philippine nationalism, to recognize the influence of foreign thinking among the region's intellectuals. However, the advance of new ideas was far more restricted in the prewar years, and the explosion of both externally based knowledge and the interchange of ideas with individuals and organizations from abroad has been primarily a postwar phenomenon.

An important element in this intellectual development was the growth of Islamic interaction between Southeast Asia and the Middle East. In this section these changes will be analyzed on a country-by-country basis, focusing on Indonesia and Malaysia in detail, with a briefer review of other countries with Muslim minorities. In the course of that analysis changes in education, literature, and religious thinking will be pointed out. However, it may first be useful to note how the Middle East has viewed the course of contemporary Islamic thinking in Southeast Asia.

As outlined in chapter 1, the prewar years saw increasing religious interaction between the two regions but a continuation of a major imbalance in influence. At no time did Southeast Asia challenge the Middle East as the fountainhead of Muslim religious thought. The postwar period has seen no major change in the religious intellectual dominance of the Middle East, but Southeast Asia is beginning to take its place in worldwide Islamic forums and greater consideration is being given the region by Middle Eastern scholars. However, the recognition of Islam in Southeast Asia by the rest of the Muslim world has been slow in coming.

It was not until 1982 that the *Index Islamicus* had a section on South and Southeast Asia, and then most of the citations were about Pakistan and India. A perusal of the *Middle East Abstracts and Index* also shows few articles referring to Southeast Asia in the 1970s and early 1980s, and the selective bibliography *The Contemporary Middle East, 1948–1973* has sections on Middle Eastern relations with the Soviet Union, the United States, the United Kingdom, France, and China, but no references to bilateral interaction with Southeast Asia.[2] A review of other books and journals from the Middle East finds an increasing number of articles on economic interaction and references to political disputes but a dearth of material on Southeast Asian Muslim religious thinking. There are no postwar Muslim writers from Southeast Asia who have achieved the prominence in the Islamic world of their religious compatriots from Arab countries, Iran, or the Indian subcontinent. Thus, there are relatively few citations crediting Islamic thinkers from the region in foreign religious material. In part, this pattern has been due to a continuing stereotypical view of the Southeast Asian Muslim as somewhat unsophisticated, overly influenced by un-Islamic local culture, and thus in need of guidance from his Middle Eastern "betters." Thus, in this chapter the increasing importance of Middle Eastern religious thinking in Southeast Asia rather than vice versa will be illustrated.

MALAYSIA

The Malaysian Muslim elite has generally been more willing to look to the Arab world for religious leadership than their Indonesian counterparts. The Middle East remains the primary source of religious ideas, the place where a high percentage of graduates of local religious schools want to go for further education, and the center of the universal brotherhood of Islam. At the same time, there continues to be some antipathy toward the perceived arrogance of Arabs and a recognition that Malaysia's situation is different from that of the Middle East. As one political spokesman stated, "Malaysian leaders are aware that in its multi-racial and multi-religious society, Islamisation as in [the Middle East] cannot be done."[3] Still, there has been strong desire to look to the Arab world for religious and language training and to Arab governments for aid in fostering religious education in Malaysia.

Education

Two primary influences of the Middle East on Malaysian education can be seen in the schooling obtained by Malays overseas and the support of education in the country by Middle Eastern governments. Cairo, Mecca, and Baghdad have long been major attractions to Malays seeking religious education abroad. In spite of often poor living conditions and food, complaints about Malaysian governmental interference and control, and inadequate preparation in Arabic, Malay students still flock to the Middle East for religious education. These conditions were exemplified by a 1985 article in the *New Straits Times* in which Malay students related that they were quite unhappy with life in student hostels in Cairo and with Kuala Lumpur's efforts to ensure that they attended classes and did not get involved in politics.[4] The Malaysian Embassy even took over responsibility of the Malay student association. Middle Eastern governments in the postwar era have helped bring Malays to educational institutions in their countries, with Al-Azhar being a major attraction. Saudi Arabia, Iraq, Iran, Kuwait, Turkey, and other states have also offered scholarships, but many of these were not in the religious field.

    Those going to the Middle East for an education have usually been of a conservative religious bent, although the government in Malaysia regards them as possible recruits for radical Islamic and political thinking (a reason that Kuala Lumpur has attempted to keep tight control over them). These students have tended to romanticize Islam in the Middle East. In the words of one visitor, "Medinah and Mecca are the only places left in the world where people still live like Muslims."[5] Both in the Middle East and back home these students have displayed an interest in expanding the role of Islam in the political and social life of Malaysia. Many have been drawn to the more conservative Parti Islam sa-Malaysia (PAS) and PAS politicians have often visited students in such centers as Al-Azhar.[6]

PAS itself has been self-admittedly strongly influenced by Arab political and religious thinking, particularly of Egyptian reformers.[7] Many of the party's ideas were also developed by the Muslim Brotherhood, Maududi, the Jama'ati of Pakistan, and Sayyed Qutb. However, many critics say that PAS members have tended to interpret individuals like Qutb and Al-Banna in especially rigid ways. PAS has expressed the general view that "Islam is a complete code for the entire individual life or rather a comprehensive way of life, spiritually or materially."[8] But it would be a serious overstatement to say that there has been a universal politicization or religious radicalization of those studying in the Middle East. In fact, as we shall see, the educational experience in Western societies has often had a more radicalizing tendency.

The impact of schooling in the Middle East can be observed throughout the Muslim religious system in Malaysia. Scholars trained in the Middle East have dominated the religious faculty of institutions of higher learning in the country. For example, in 1988–89 at the Universiti Malaya's Fakulti Syariah, thirteen of seventeen faculty had some education at Al-Azhar and three at Baghdad; in the Fakulti Usuluddin (Knowledge of Islamic Tenets), ten were educated at Al-Azhar, five in Riyadh, two in Baghdad, and two elsewhere in the Middle East; and in the Fakulti Kursus Tamaddun Islam (Islamic Civilization) four of seven were taught at Al-Azhar. These figures exclude tutors, and numbers may exceed 100 percent because of schooling at more than one location.[9] A similar pattern has existed at the Universiti Kebangsaan, where in 1984–85 all the professors had had an Al-Azhar education, as did a majority of the religious faculty.[10] However, those with Ph.D.'s at Universiti Malaya and Universiti Kebangsaan came from Western universities, which, of course offered these degrees.

It is also interesting to peruse the reading list for courses taught in the Islamic faculties of both institutions. Many of the seminal spokesmen of the Islamic revival in the Middle East were on these lists, including Maududi, Qutb, and Khurshid Ahmad, as well as Western authors on Islam such as Maxine Rodinson and Charles Hamilton. The curriculum of the International Islamic University contains a number of modern Muslim thinkers such as Al-Afghani, Sayyid Ahmad Khan, Ameer Ali, and Iqbal. The Muslim College at Klang also has had close links with Al-Azhar, and there was once even a suggestion to call it "The al-Azharite Muslim College of Malaya."

At a lower educational level, the Arabic schools, or madrasah, have often been founded by Arabs. Many of the teachers have either been educated in the Middle East or were Arabs themselves. Historically, Arabic-language teachers have been from Egypt, although there have been recent efforts to work out programs to bring Malays to Saudi Arabia for Arabic-language training. This importation of Arabs has been part of a long process of attempting to improve religious and language teaching at the secondary level. For example, one observer of Islamic education in Kelantan notes that in 1956 graduates from Cairo and Al-Azhar were employed to upgrade local religious schools.[11]

It is important for local religious teachers to show their ties to the Middle East. It provides legitimacy and an aura of learning that no other experience can match. As Judith Nagata put it, "In the chain of scholarship, connections with the Middle East take precedence over all others, and the aura of the Holy Land is a powerful one. In the absence of a personal guru/disciple or kinship/marriage relationship, the *isnad* [chain of religious authority] can be established by a university degree such as one from Cairo's Al-Azhar."[12]

Middle Eastern countries have made efforts to aid education in Malaysia more directly. Many of these efforts, such as the provision of Turkish lecturers at the Universiti Teknoloji Malaysia or Saudi aid to Mara colleges and to the Universiti Kebangsaan to improve faculty and equipment, have had no specific religious purpose. Other foreign-supported activity has been to foster Islamic education in general without defining its content. This approach can best be exemplified by the multinational support for the Islamic University by such diverse countries as Saudi Arabia, Libya, Turkey, and Bangladesh. A third type of support may be called underwriting more individual national interests, for example, Saudi funds for religious education or the Libyan-Arab Cultural Centre in Kuala Lumpur with its library, information center, and conference hall.

In sum, Malays have long sought religious education in the Middle East. In the postwar era this pattern continued, aided by Arab states providing scholarships and programs tailored for Southeast Asian students. This chain of scholarship in the religious realm reaches down to the villages. However, another increasingly important set of religious links has also developed, which will be explored more thoroughly in the Indonesian section. Suffice it to state here that this other linkage has been through Western educational institutions, particularly in the United Kingdom, the United States, and Australia. Southeast Asians studying in these countries have come in contact with Muslims from other Islamic countries and have become familiar with the writings of revivalist Middle Eastern writers. When combined with the often traumatic experience of living in a non-Muslim society, this has often increased these students' Malay-Muslim identity and radicalized them religiously.

Religious Books and Articles

This work in part is a result of my own observations of changes in the kind of religious literature available in Malaysia over the years. While in Malaya/Malaysia in 1963–64, I was acquiring books on Islam for the University of Wisconsin. At that time, there was little writing by contemporary foreign authors on Islam available in the bookshops other than that by Indonesian scholars, particularly Hamka. In the 1960s there were a few Indonesian translations of Maududi's works, but these were the exception to the rule. Even a review of books printed in Malay in Malaysia from 1971 to 1975 finds no works by Middle Eastern writers such as Qutb, Maududi, or Shariati.[13]

The penetration of modern Islamic thinking into Malaysia is different today. Even a brief perusal of contemporary missionary magazines, required reading in religious faculties, and books available in Malay translation now presents a wide range of contemporary Middle Eastern religious material. The works of Shariati, Qutb, Al-Banna, Turabi, Maududi, Sheikh Mohammed Al Ghazali, Maryam Jameelah, and others have been regularly quoted in books on Islam or in periodicals such as *Dakwah*, *Risalah*, or *Al-Nahdah*. Students and faculty in religion departments are at least conversant, if not always in sympathy, with much of this contemporary literature. Malaysian scholars argue that they have a better knowledge of both Arabic and English than their Indonesian counterparts and that this opens more doors to the Islamic world. Malaysia has become an active participant in the worldwide Islamic dialogues that have sought to interpret Islam in its contemporary setting.

INDONESIA

As discussed in chapter 1, Indonesia experienced considerably more intellectual interaction with the Middle East in the prewar era than did Malaysia. However, the war and its aftermath formed temporary barriers to the continuation of this pattern. During their occupation of the Indies, the Japanese were suspicious of both Pan-Islam and the influence of the Middle East and local Arabs on Indonesian Muslims.[14] Initially, there were attempts to make Islam "Asian-centered" and to substitute the "Greater East Asian Co-Prosperity Sphere" for Pan-Islam. Apparently, the Japanese were particularly worried about the influence of the Arab minority on their fellow believers in the Indies. In the first year of the occupation, the Japanese military authorities attempted to ban the teaching of Arabic in all religious schools and made efforts to curtail Arab schools. In part due to Japanese pressure and in part as a result of growing Indonesian self-identity, the war years saw a movement away from the use of Arabic in prayers and a greater use of the vernacular.

In the initial postwar years, contact with the Middle East was limited by domestic conflict, first during efforts to gain independence from the Dutch from 1945 to 1949 and then in a decade of civil strife. The long war for independence isolated Indonesia from the rest of the world, with the exception of a small number of representatives abroad. The civil disturbances of the 1950s were particularly destabilizing in Sumatra, West Java, and East Indonesia. Foreign travel and study were inhibited by severely limited funds and unsettled political conditions in large parts of the islands.[15] The bloody aftermath of the attempted coup in 1965 further unsettled domestic conditions. However, after the mid-1960s, internal conditions were more peaceful and a stronger economy provided a foundation for Indonesians' increased interest in worldwide Islamic affairs. The development of intellectual contacts can be seen most prominently in the advance of contempo-

rary Middle Eastern religious writers into Indonesia and the continued importance of obtaining religious education in Arab universities.

Publications

When commenting on the Iranian Revolution's impact on Indonesia,
M. Nasir Tamara remarked on the increase in translations into Bahasa
Indonesia of Iranian writers such as Bani Sadr and Ali Shariati.[16] This
change was only part of a major growth in translations of books and
articles dealing with Muslim issues by Middle Eastern authors. Writing in 1986, Tamara observed:

> There have never been so many books published and so many articles
> printed as in the past six years. Not just books of Indonesian scholars
> and intellectuals but also translations of foreign works and this time not
> only from the Western world but mostly from Islamic countries in the
> Middle East. . . .
>
> Most of these books are about Islam. There have always been books on
> Islam published in Indonesia and they sell well. But the books published
> now are not just about Islamic rituals, e.g., how to pray correctly, but
> also deal with issues that concern the Muslim polity, about Islamic soci-
> ety and state, economics and problems of equality.[17]

The author notes the translations of Sayyed Qutb, the former leader of
the Muslim Brotherhood, and Ali Shariati, intellectual forefather of the
Iranian Revolution. But it is obvious that other seminal writers on the
Islamic resurgence, such as Maududi, Iqbal, Al Ghazali, and Hasan Al-
Banna, have also been widely published. These authors have also been
frequently covered in periodicals such as *Tempo, Dakwah, Prisma,* and
Mizan.

The evidence of these writers' popularity is apparent from a review
of the number and variety of translations of Middle Eastern authors
during the 1980s. For example, the *Diskusi Buku Islam,* which lists
books published in Indonesia on religious subjects, notes twelve
Bahasa translations of Qutb from 1982 to 1986, ten of Maududi, six of
Shariati from 1983 to 1985, and three of Hasan Al-Banna during that
period.[18] Another 1987 bibliography of Muslim books published in
Indonesia since 1945 lists eleven books by Qutb translated in the
1980s, fourteen by Maududi, all but three published in the first half of

the 1980s, and eight each by Shariati and Al-Banna, all from the 1980s.[19] In many cases, there was more than one translation of a particular work, although the transliteration of the title often clouded the exact nature of a particular book.

Some of the popularity of these religious translations can be attributed to the limited ability of the Indonesian Muslim masses to read the originals in Arabic. A good reading knowledge of Arabic script has increasingly become the province of the religiously learned and best Muslim schools.[20] As such, it gives further legitimacy to religious teachers, but at present it is a barrier to the growing number of Indonesians interested in the new ideas coming from the Middle East.

It is difficult to assess the impact of these writers and their concepts on the Indonesian intellectual elite. It is possible to observe the extent to which authors such as Qutb, Shariati, or Maududi are quoted or footnoted in religious treatises. Hamka, Indonesia's most renowned postwar Muslim writer, urged Indonesians to read thinkers such as Qutb and Maududi.[21] Muhammad Natsir, president of the Dewan Dawa Islamiyah and one-time Muslim party leader, was one of the sponsors of studies in honor of Maududi.[22] Finally, a perusal of the syllabi of departments of religion in Indonesian institutions shows the prevalence of writers such as Qutb and Al Ghazali.[23] However much of these writings is internalized is open to question, and often the translated selections used in these institutions are of the more traditional type.

In fact, some Indonesians argue that all too often local Muslim scholars look to the less theologically sophisticated or more ideological works of contemporary Middle Eastern authors. This lack is attributed to the limited scope of the Indonesian language, difficulties in translating from Arabic to Indonesian, and the weaknesses in religious training. Thus, one Indonesian scholar argues that the local Muslim community has adopted only M. Abduh's thoughts on *fiqh* (Islamic jurisprudence) and not his more fundamental concepts, "which is due to the limited intellectual capabilities and traditions of this community."[24] Although this limitation is true of the Muslim community as a whole, it is important to stress that there are many highly sophisticated Indonesians more than capable of understanding the intricacies of contemporary religious thinking.

One of the interesting facets of this influence from the Middle East has been the penetration of Shi'i ideas. In this instance we are not assessing the impact of the Iranian Revolution itself but to the concepts inherent in Shi'i world views. Southeast Asia is Sunni with a predilection to the Shafi'i school of law. Shi'i concepts have been found attractive primarily by a small intellectual elite, and most Muslims are indifferent to differences between Shi'i and Sunni. Within the aforementioned circle of intellectuals, certain Shi'i concepts have been particularly attractive, including what is perceived to be a more rational means of theological analysis. Nurcholish Madjid wrote in an interview in *Panji Masyarakat*, "One of the traditional characteristics of Shia intellectualism is the strength of takwil, the strength metaphorical interpretation concerning religious teachings. Just look at the writings of Ali Syari'ati [Shariati]. That is only intellectualization, deductive thinking, because Shia is more speculative than Sunni. And because of that, also more abstractive and receptive to philosophy. That is the reason at this time the Shia group is flowering."[25] Nurcholish went on to say that he rejected the absolute authority of "Khoumeini-ism." He referred to the rather eclectic nature of Shi'i thought in Indonesia as "Gado-Gado" Shi'ism—Gado-Gado being a mixed Indonesian salad. However, he also stated that he was not sure precisely what Shi'ism was in Indonesia, although the youth were attracted to it by a romanticism that identified with the revolutionary Iranian leader.[26]

Beyond the impact of the Revolution itself, the influence of one of its intellectual forefathers, Ali Shariati, has been considerable. This influence is not because of Shi'i concepts as much as it is because of Shariati's views of an egalitarian Muslim society and attacks on corrupt religious leadership. In the words of one of his Indonesian translators, "Muslim intellectuals will have a meaning and function only when they place themselves constantly among the masses; informing them, guiding them and carrying out with them a revival towards a better life and a better Islam."[27] Shariati also expressed what some Indonesians perceive to be the more speculative thinking and use of metaphorical interpretation attributed to Shi'ism. At the same time, the intellectual influence of the other Middle Eastern maverick, Libyan leader Khaddafi, is almost universally described as minimal at best. Indonesians interviewed observed that those receiving an education in Libya would not officially be able to teach in Indonesia because of government rules.

It is also intriguing to look at this penetration of modern Muslim ideas from the Middle East by identifying many of the transmitters. Two observations can be made about a significant percentage of the articles and books in this regard. First, sources are frequently not Middle Eastern writers or even fellow believers but Western writers on Islam. Regularly footnoted have been Dutch writers such as C. Snouck Hurgronje, A. R. Kern, C. Lekkerkerker, and D. W. J. Drewes as well as North American and other European authors such as H. A. R. Gibb, Wilfred Cantwell Smith, and Maxine Rodinson. Next, although the articles may be in Bahasa, the footnotes are often from English, not from the original Arabic sources.[28]

The explanation for these patterns may be found in several aspects of contemporary Indonesian Islamic scholarship. One is the limited number of Arabic readers and the extent to which English is now challenging the traditional role of Arabic even in the *pesantren* (Islamic religious school).[29] Further, it is significant that among the most well-known interpreters of the Islamic revival in the Middle East are individuals educated not only in Indonesian religious schools and Al-Azhar but in the West as well. Among these well-known writers are Harun Nasution (educated at Cairo University and recipient of a Ph.D. in Islamic philosophy from McGill University), Nurcholish Madjid (who received his degree in Islamic philosophy from the University of Chicago), Alfian, a political science Ph.D. from the University of Wisconsin), M. Amien Rais (a graduate of Gadja Mada, a Notre Dame alumnus, and a Ph.D. recipient from the University of Chicago), Imaduddin (educated at the University of Iowa and the University of Chicago and at times compared with Shariati), and Ahmad Syafii Maarif (also a Ph.D. from the University of Chicago). An Indonesian conference on Islam and the social sciences held in the early 1980s found a quarter of the participants had degrees from institutions in North America, Europe, and Asia. They had attended universities in Wisconsin, Illinois, Pennsylvania, New York, Connecticut, Massachusetts, Tennessee, Iowa, Indiana, the Netherlands, and Japan.[30]

These men appear to have been less interested in continuing the narrower traditional Sharia education of the religious education of Indonesian Islamic schools and Al-Azhar and more involved in the ethical and contemporary issues often articulated by writers such as Shariati and Maududi. They presented to the Indonesian public the ideas of these Middle Eastern authors in part through the prism of their Western education. Even among Indonesian students in the Middle East, who have often been wary of Western-educated scholars of Islam, these men are widely read through Muslim publications from home. Thus, as in Malaysia, without denigrating the importance of the Middle Eastern educational connection, it can be argued that major Indonesian transmissions for new ideas from that area were not only Al-Azhar and Baghdad but also the University of Chicago, the University of California at Los Angeles, the Australian National University, the University of Glasgow, and McGill University. In these places individuals encountered faculty and fellow students knowledgeable about modern currents from the Middle East, and they transmitted these ideas back to Southeast Asia.

Middle Eastern Education

Some observers believe that the influence of Al-Azhar is less prominent today than it once was, particularly in Java.[31] However, in the prewar years the educational institutions of Cairo, particularly Al-Azhar, played a major role in influencing Indonesian Islamic education.[32] A number of prominent prewar and early postwar religious leaders received their training in Egypt. A sizable number of them fell under the spell of modernism and the Muslim Brotherhood, among them Muhammad Rashidi (first minister of religious affairs in independent Indonesia), Kahir Muzakkir (founder of Sunan Kalijaga in Jogjakarta), and Professor Fu'ad Fakhruddin (scholar and diplomat). The first two had the opportunity to interact with Sayyed Qutb. These men and others were largely responsible for upgrading Indonesian Islamic education.

In the postindependence era, especially in the 1960s, a number of Indonesians who were to become influential in Islamic affairs came to Cairo. It was a period of considerable intellectual ferment with the ideas of the Brotherhood, Nasser, Third World ideologies, Western political and cultural literature, and men such as Qutb and Maududi challenging the minds of these young students. A great number of these ideas were still prevalent in the next decades, with the addition of a greater interest in Khoumeini and Shariati. Nevertheless, many argue that there was both a greater intellectual vitality at places like

Al-Azhar in the 1960s and that today's Indonesian students are as a whole less capable than their predecessors. Certainly there was a marked increase of students in the seventies and eighties. However, Cairo has remained a place where Southeast Asian students come in contact with new religious and secular ideas that are not always viewed with favor by their respective governments.

In the 1980s there was still a significant number of Indonesian students in Cairo and the Middle East. In 1987 there were 722 in Egypt, 585 of whom were studying in Al-Azhar. The largest number of Indonesian students that year were in Saudi Arabia (904) where scholarships were available, with twenty-seven in Libya, thirty-two in Iran, twenty-one in Syria, ten in Sudan, nine in Jordan, eight in Iraq, seven in Turkey, and two in Algeria.[33] Many were not involved in religious studies. Generally, Southeast Asian students have felt freer of local government restrictions in Egypt than in Saudi Arabia. However, the Indonesian Embassy in Cairo has watched these students with care out of fear of possible political deviations and has dissolved a number of student organizations in part because they did not accept the Panchasila as their sole ideology. This was after what the embassy called "maximal guidance."[34] It is important to remember that while a majority of long-term Indonesian students in Cairo visit Mecca at least once during their sojourn, making the haj from Cairo necessitates Indonesian Embassy clearance, which might be withheld for political reasons.

Student life in postwar Al-Azhar has not been easy. Not only have there been complaints in Egypt from religious and secular sources about the alleged intellectual decline at the university, but the number of failures among Indonesian students has been high and living conditions poor. Many Indonesians have found their Arabic wanting and home degrees unacceptable. Often coming from poor rural families, they feel discriminated against by the Al-Azhar administration and students.[35] Nor have the Indonesian students been satisfied with the quality of their education at Al-Azhar, and unlike many of their predecessors of the sixties and seventies, they do not see their degree there as leading to a graduate career in the West.[36]

It is also interesting to note the relatively small number of Indonesian students doing graduate work in Cairo. In 1987 there were forty postgraduate students at Al-Azhar, and from 1981 to 1988 only nine

Ph.D.'s and twenty-four M.A.'s were completed at Egyptian universities. Of course, not all of these graduates were pursuing religious studies. As in the Malaysian case, many of the more influential writers on Islam combined their Cairo educations with advanced study in the West in nonreligious areas of interest.

The problems and character of the students returning from the Middle East do not diminish their impact in Indonesia. It may be argued, though, that they will likely be more influential at the local level rather than in the national religious dialogues where their more Western-educated brethren tend to dominate.[37] It is through their roles in rural pesantren and "old boy" organizations that they have made their impact. Abaza has observed:

> It is thus possible to argue that in contrast to the previous generations of Azhar graduates who reached significant posts as technocrats and who participated in the Islamic discourse within the nation state (although in an ambivalent manner) . . . most of the Azhar graduates of the generation of the eighties seem to rather end up working in the village community, pesantren type of activities or as preachers and mosque officials. In fact, one could here argue that the majority of Azhar graduates evolve in different spheres of functions than the European-trained scholars.[38]

Beyond this differentiation, interviews with Modernist religious spokesmen elicit the view that while Middle Eastern religious education for Indonesians remains of importance, particularly at the local level, it is of declining influence. They refer to the greater impact of Western-trained Indonesian Islamic scholars, particularly on national issues and employment positions.

However, Arab educational influence at the local and national levels also originates from Arab scholars and businessmen living in Indonesia. In 1980–81 there were twenty-one Egyptian teachers in the various Indonesian Islamic universities, and in 1986–88 there were twenty-seven such products of Al-Azhar throughout the archipelago.[39] Arabs have also been important educationally with regard to their ownership of bookstores and private Arabic language libraries. Culturally, they help transmit the Arabic language, poetry, and music and generally provide important lines of contact with educational centers of the Middle East. In places like Sulawesi, where Al-Azhar graduates have been particularly prominent, they aid in attracting local students to further study in Cairo. Yet, as mentioned, there is a certain antagonism against the Arabs because of their lifestyle, their perceived arrogance, and the politics of their homelands. This attitude is more prevalent in Indonesia than in Malaysia.

MINORITY POPULATIONS

Generally speaking, Muslim minorities in Southeast Asia have been more isolated from external intellectual ideas of all sorts than have their counterparts in Malaysia and Indonesia. However, even here it is necessary to differentiate among the various national groups. Those from Vietnam and Burma have been most limited in their contacts with the rest of the Islamic world, due in part to internal strife and in part to the authoritarian nature of their respective governments.[40] Muslim minorities in the Philippines and Thailand have, for the most part, lived in regions outside the major centers of commerce and international interaction, both being concentrated in rural areas of the far south of their respective countries. At the same time, the leadership of these minorities and those living in the capital cities did develop international interactions with fellow Muslims. But comparatively fewer members of any of these minorities have been educated in the universities of the Middle East and the percentage of pilgrims from these areas to Mecca has been considerably smaller than from other Muslim countries in the region.[41]

Singapore's Muslim minority has traditionally been more aware of external Islamic activities because of its urban nature and the presence of Muslims from the Arab and South Asian regions. Local Malay Muslims have tended to be more isolated and have been both economically less advantaged and more poorly educated than other Singaporeans. The need to go to secular schools for economic advancement and the limited programs of Muslim educational institutions have also been problems.[42] Still, there is a wide range of Islamic literature available and approximately 1,000 pilgrims make the haj annually.

The Philippines and Thailand have been more directly penetrated by Muslim thought from the Middle East than has Burma or Vietnam. In the Philippines, not only have secessionist leaders interacted with organizations such as the OIC and even lived in friendly countries

Table 8. Number of Moro Students Awarded Scholarships by
Muslim States

Country	1977	1978	1979	1980	1981
Egypt	10	17	7	1	—
Indonesia	—	4	1	—	—
Kuwait	3	2	4	2	3
Libya	1	—	4	—	—
Saudi Arabia	55	54	82	31	57
UAE	—	—	4	2	3
Total	69	77	102	36	63

such as Libya, but Filipino scholars of Islam such as Cesar Majul and
Michael Matsura were frequently involved in international academic
conferences in the West and Middle East. More than other minority
groups, Filipinos have availed themselves of the opportunity for religious education in the Middle East, particularly Egypt. Private organizations and governments have provided hundreds of scholarships
for Moros to attend institutions such as Al-Azhar and the Islamic
University of Medina.[43]

There has also been an increase in the number of Filipino Muslims
making the pilgrimage to Mecca, due in part to the establishment by
presidential decree of the Philippine Pilgrimage Authority in 1978. It
quickly raised the number of pilgrims from 1,022 to 1,801, still a
comparatively small number.[44]

Among the large volume of workers in the Middle East from the
Philippines, a small percentage of Filipino Muslims had some interaction with other Muslims there. Filipinos, particularly those residing in
urban areas, have also been targets of external religious organizations. Like other Muslim populations in Southeast Asia, Muslims in
the Philippines have seen a growing amount of Muslim literature
from abroad. For example, at the end of the 1970s, Filipino Muslims
first became exposed to Shi'i intellectual thought through the availability of Shi'i literature in the Philippines provided by the Iranian
Embassy, the Ministry of National Guidance of Iran, the Shariati
Foundation, and the Islamic Propagation Organization.[45] This apparently did not have much impact on the Muslim masses but was at

least of passing interest to younger religious leaders, many of whom had been educated in the Arab world.

Overall, this contact has had a profound effect on the Filipino Muslim population. Asiri Abubakar has observed that the Muslim resurgence in the republic has been due to

> (1) an increase in contact with the *Ulama* (religious teachers) and other learned Muslim visitors from the Arab world; (2) an increase in the number of Moros (Muslims) going on the haj (pilgrimage to Mecca); (3) an increase in study opportunities in various Islamic centres in the world; (4) active participation in meetings of various international Islamic groups; (5) return of hundreds of Muslim students from abroad; (6) establishment of more *Madaris* (religious schools) in the countryside; (7) visits to Moroland (Philippines) of officials from the Muslim world; and (8) international press conferences and coverage on the on-going war in Mindanao and the abuses committed by some military personnel in the region.[46]

The Thai minority situation has been similar to that of the Philippines, although the Moros have received more attention from the Middle East, and neighboring Malaysia has been an important transmission path for new Islamic concepts to enter the region. Separatist groups in Thailand have developed long-term contacts with the Arab world, receiving cultural as well as financial support from the Middle East. Personnel from these organizations and workers from southern Thailand residing in the Middle East have used the opportunity to develop a better knowledge and understanding of Islam. An increasing amount of foreign Islamic literature is finding its way into the region, often coming through Malaysia. Muslim countries have provided scholarships to local Muslims who have gone abroad to study in Egypt, Saudi Arabia, Pakistan, Libya, Kuwait, Syria, the Sudan, and Iraq.[47] There has been an increase of Thai pilgrims going to Mecca, although government officials have reportedly been concerned about politically dangerous influences. Accordingly, they have established surveillance programs in the Middle East to check on pilgrims and students in the region. As seen in chapter 3, there is some possible Iranian Shi'i influence, but it appears to be limited and, unlike the Philippines, has not been influenced by the presence of local Iranian students. Finally, as in Bangkok, there is a small but somewhat sophisticated Muslim populace in Thailand that has developed more international intellectual contacts than some of their more rural counterparts.

CONCLUSION

From this brief assessment of Islamic interaction between the Middle East and Southeast Asia it is possible to draw some conclusions.

1. Middle Eastern religious ideas still dominate the exchange between the two regions. There is relatively little influence by Southeast Asian Muslim intellectuals on the rest of the Muslim world.

2. The past several decades have seen a significant increase in the number and variety of contemporary Middle Eastern authors read and translated into Malay-Indonesian. The most prominent of these have been Qutb, Maududi, Shariati, Al-Banna, Iqbal, Al Ghazali, Al-Afghani, and other spokesmen of less traditional Muslim thinking.

3. However, although these external influences have become increasingly important, the dominant religious thinking of the region tends to remain indigenous in nature. There is also some question as to the extent to which the general Muslim community of Southeast Asia understands the more sophisticated elements of the religious thinking of these foreign authors.

4. Religious education in the Middle East, and in Cairo in particular, remains a major source of Muslim thought in Southeast Asia. Especially in Indonesia, it tends to have its major influence at the local level—in mosques and religious schools.

5. Increasingly, the transmission path for contemporary Middle Eastern Muslim ideas is coming from Indonesians and Malaysians with local or Middle Eastern religious schooling but advanced Western degrees.

6. Muslim minority populations have been comparatively more isolated from external intellectual currents than their coreligionists in Indonesia and Malaysia, although their leadership has developed considerable contact with the outside world and educational opportunities in the Middle East have increased.

7. Overall, Southeast Asian Muslims have become an integral part of the worldwide Muslim intellectual resurgence and are gaining the tools to provide their own interpretations of Islam to the *ummah*.

Chapter 6

REVIVAL AND INTERACTION

 In chapter 5, a Filipino Muslim listed a number of factors that he believed had aided the Islamic resurgence in that republic. He included aspects of the interaction between Filipino Muslims and those from abroad. In this chapter the extent to which interaction between Muslims in the Middle East and those in Southeast Asia has fostered the Islamic resurgence in the latter will be further detailed. This interaction has not been the only force responsible for the much-publicized growth in Islamic identity in the region. Other factors have been the challenge of modernization in previously largely rural populations; efforts by political leaders, parties, and governments to manipulate religious symbols; conflicts with non-Muslim domestic elements; the development of a more knowledgeable and sophisticated Muslim elite; and a sense among many Muslims that solutions offered by the West to national and personal problems have been largely incapable of meeting their needs. However, there have also been extremely important external forces at work. In this chapter the impact of those forces will be assessed.

ECONOMIC

We have seen the limited correlation between the common religious affinity of the two Muslim regions and economic interaction. Workers from Southeast Asia to Saudi Arabia, Iraq, Kuwait, and other places have been largely from non-Muslim societies, investment has been low compared with that developed in Western countries, and economic decision makers in the Arab world would appear to have given little consideration to religious similarities with their Southeast Asian brethren. But none of these factors means that economic forces have not played an important indirect and direct role in vitalizing the Islamic resurgence in the East.

Indirectly, the very wealth and perceived power resulting from the petrodollar explosion after the early 1970s increased the sense of pride and Islamic identity among Southeast Asian Muslims. For the first time in the modern era, the Western states seemed to display fear, if not respect, for the ability of at least one part of the Islamic world to endanger their vital national interests. Although not particularly enamored of the life-styles of many wealthy Arabs, Southeast Asians saw Western Europe, North America, and Japan recognize a new major economic player, led by Saudi Arabia, the home of the holy cities. Within the region, it was also obvious that the alleged pro-Arab foreign policies and greater attention to the needs of their Muslim minorities of countries like the Philippines were a reflection of their worry over possible cutoffs of petroleum.

More directly, the newfound wealth of the Middle Eastern countries gave them the ability to aid their fellow Muslims in Southeast Asia in the religious realm. This aid was not simply the result of events of the early 1970s in the Middle East as there had been important examples of support for Islamic causes by states in that region prior to that period, particularly by Saudi Arabia. However, after 1973 there were significant increases in scholarships to universities in the Middle East, including many for Islamic studies, in funds for religious education and institutions, in aid to private and public Muslim religious organizations, and in the introduction of subsidized religious literature into the region. These trends were especially important in countries with Muslim minorities where there was relatively little traditional governmental support for Islamic needs. Even in places like Malaysia, though, where there has been a long history of state aid to Islam, Middle Eastern finances helped to develop innovative projects such as the International Islamic University.

POLITICAL

Preceding chapters have underscored the developing interest and involvement of both regions in the other's foreign and domestic problems. Although the role played by Southeast Asian states in Middle Eastern issues has tended to be peripheral, it has given their people a greater sense of being part of the wider Islamic community. This consciousness has been achieved through speaking out for fellow Muslims over the Palestine issue, expressing concern regarding intra-Muslim disputes in the Middle East, attempting mediation in some disputes, and working with other Muslim states in international organizations. Thus, though in all probability Middle Eastern governments do not see the Southeast Asians as considerably important to their cause except to show the unity of the *ummah*, from the perspective of many people of Malaysia and Indonesia involvement is sufficient proof of their new international role.

Major questions exist about the impact and extent of Middle Eastern governmental involvement in Southeast Asian activities in some issues and obvious cases of influence in others. In the latter case, it would appear that the efforts of Libya, Saudi Arabia, and the OIC were significant in forcing the Philippines to attempt to reach an amicable agreement with its Muslim minority and of more minimal importance concerning the problems of other Muslim minorities in the region. In their efforts to aid their fellow Muslims, Arab states have increased their support of religious education, institutions, organizations, and propaganda in all these states. In the process, as remarked by the aforementioned Filipino Muslim, the Islamic resurgence was vitalized. Middle Eastern allies also provided the possibility for many of these separatists to find a home and a forum abroad where they came into contact with other Muslim activists.

It is far more difficult to ascertain the extent of activity, and thus influence, of Middle Eastern states in the domestic politics of Muslim majority states. As we have observed, there have been veiled accusations of clandestine Libyan and Iranian involvement with opposition elements in Malaysia and Indonesia and public financial support for Muslim organizations by Libya and the Saudis. There also has been distribution of literature, now better controlled by local governments, by Iranian government and private sources. While in all probability there have been limited clandestine operations, such activities are likely to have had only marginal influence on individuals and some small fringe radical groups. Certainly none of these organizations has successfully challenged the political and religious establishments in either Malaysia or Indonesia.

The indirect impact of radical Middle Eastern governments and organizations has probably been of greater importance to the development of the resurgence. On the one hand, there have been limiting consequences such as Southeast Asian governments' attempts to control local religious opponents by manipulating fear of radical Islam. This fear has been fostered by raising the specter of deviant Islam aided from abroad as a force intent on subverting true belief. On the other hand, the Iranian Revolution and the acts and rhetoric of radical Middle Eastern organizations have vitalized both fringe groups in Southeast Asia seeking fundamental political and religious changes and a wider audience attracted by the symbol of the Iranian Revolution. There well may have been an emulative effect among local fringe elements who have seen small radical groups in Lebanon and Egypt profoundly affect both domestic and international issues. Also, we have seen the extent to which the Revolution has been perceived by many Indonesian and Malaysian Muslims as an example of an anti-imperialist, anti-establishment, anti-secular victory of Islam. It can be argued that the influence of the radical groups has been of only tangential importance, while the long-term indirect impact of the Revolution on the Islamic revival in Southeast Asia has been far more sweeping. The longer effect has not been in terms of a strong desire to establish another Iran but a revitalizing of religious identity and belief in the ultimate achievement of a society built on Islamic principles.

Finally, the involvement of Southeast Asian governments in international Islamic organizations has contributed to the resurgence by giving their people a sense of real participation in the activities of the ummah. One can see from references in the press and speeches of political and religious leaders that there has been considerable pride in having indigenous officers of such organs as the OIC and WAMY, seeing government officials speaking about issues of importance to the Muslim world at the Islamic foreign ministers' conferences, and hosting a myriad of Muslim private and governmental conferences. From time to time, these organizations have also provided more tangible contributions such as scholarships, aid to religious education, and opportunities to interact with other Muslims.

INTELLECTUAL

In chapter 5, the considerable increase in Islamic intellectual interaction during the postwar era was described. Two aspects of this growth are of particular importance in vitalizing the Islamic re-surgence in Southeast Asia. First, we have seen how when Southeast Asians have gone abroad they have come in contact with the new ideas that have formed the basis for the worldwide Muslim re-surgence. Contacts with contemporary Islamic thinking have oc-curred in more traditional places such as Saudi Arabia during the pilgrimage and Middle Eastern universities such as Al-Azhar, Baghdad, and Medina. But of equal and perhaps greater importance has been the influence of faculty and fellow Muslim students in West-ern institutions of higher learning in the United States, Canada, Great Britain, and Australia. In the latter type of contact, Southeast Asian Muslims often have been introduced to some of the most influential seminal writing of the resurgence and have become transmission paths for their ideas into their homelands.

A second significant factor has been the wide range of contempo-rary Muslim literature finding its way into Southeast Asia. Through the original languages, English and Malay/Indonesian translations, and explanatory articles, the works of Shariati, Maududi, Qutb, and others have reached bookstores, religious schools, Muslim student organizations, and universities. From these precincts their ideas have been reinterpreted to meet the needs of Southeast Asians seeking Islamic answers to indigenous problems. This is not to argue that the Islamic revival in Southeast Asia is simply a reaction to external events and ideas. It has deep local roots. However, there have also been major intellectual contributions to religious thinking in the re-gion from these contemporary Middle Eastern writers.

We can expect this interaction to continue. But it is also probable that Southeast Asian governments will attempt to contain what they perceive to be destabilizing religious ideas. Some have already taken action by limiting literature distributed by embassies (particularly Ira-nian), controlling where students go abroad for their education and what their activities are overseas, censoring deviant religious mate-rial, and issuing regular warnings regarding dangerous religious ideas and organizations. Nevertheless, the growth of communica-tions, the nature of today's global intellectual community, and in-creasing sophistication in religious thought all lend credence to the belief that Southeast Asian Muslims are now firmly involved in the worldwide Islamic resurgence.

Notes

1. For early trade between the Middle East, India, and Southeast Asia, see A. Reid, *Southeast Asia in the Age of Commerce: The Lands Below the Winds*; K. Chauduri, "Indonesia in the Early Seaborne Trade of the Indian Ocean"; and O. Evangelista, "Some Aspects of the History of Islam in Southeast Asia." Evangelista noted that there were those who told of an Arab community in Canton as far back as the third century. For assessments of the arrival of Islam in Southeast Asia, see A. H. Johns, "Islam in Southeast Asia"; W. Kraus, "Islam in Thailand"; H. de Graaf and T. Pigeaud, *De Eerste Moslimisme Vorstendommen op Java*; M. B. Hooker, ed., *Islam in South-East Asia*; and U. Tjandrasasmita, "The Arrival and Expansion of Islam in Indonesia in Relation to Southeast Asia."

2. See Reid, "Sixteenth-Century Turkish Influence in Western Indonesia," and H. A. Suminto, "Relations between the Ottoman Empire and the Muslim Kingdoms of the Malay-Indonesian Archipelago."

3. For an interesting view of even Kurdish influence on Indonesian Muslims at that time, see M. van Bruinessan, "Bukankah Orang Kurdi yan Mengistlainkan Indonesia?" and "Tarekat Qadiriyah dan Ilmu Syeikh Qadir Jilani di India, Kurdistan, dan Indonesia."

4. *Malayan Yearbook, 1939* (Singapore: Government Printing Office, 1939).

5. *Statistical Pocket Book of Indonesia, 1957* (Jakarta: Biro Pusat Statistik, 1957).

6. For discussions of nineteenth-century Dutch attitudes, see W. Roff, "South-East Asian Islam in the Nineteenth Century," and Suminto, *Politik Islam Hindia Belanda*. An example of missionary attitudes can be seen in G. Simon, "Pan-Islamism in Malaysia." For details on the haj from Indonesia since 1920 see H. Mursyidi, *Sumuran Harahap Lintasan Sejarah Perjalanan Jemaah Haji Indonesia*.

7. M. Williams, *Communism, Religion, and Revolt in Bantem*, 91, 98.

8. Roff, "South-East Asian Islam," 172.

9. K. Kamarun, "Sejarah Haji di Malaysia."

10. Netherland East Indies, *Indische Verslag, 1931* (Batavia, Indonesia: Landsrukerij, 1930). Also see J. Vredenbregt, "The Haddj," *Bijdragen Tot de Land- Taal-en Volkenkunde.*

11. D. van der Muelen, *Don't You Hear the Thunder?*, 114.

12. Roff, "Indonesian and Malay Students in Cairo in the 1920s," 73–74.

13. Ibid., 74.

14. Ibid.

15. M. Natsir, "Masa depan Hubungan Indonesia."

16. F. Abdullah, *Radical Malay Politics*, 54–55.

17. The best study of nineteenth-century activities of the Ottoman Empire regarding Southeast Asia is to be found in Reid, "Nineteenth Century Pan-Islam in Indonesia and Malaysia."

18. Quoted in ibid., 270.

19. For an excellent analysis of the Achenese problem, see Reid, *The Contest for North Sumatra.*

20. Reid, "Nineteenth Century Pan-Islam," 280–81.

21. "Godsdienstig advises," *Indische Gids* 37, no. 2 (1915): 1781.

22. "Pers Oversicht," *Koloniaal Tijdschrift* 5, no. 1 (1916): 370.

23. Among the best analyses of Pan-Islam in Malaya are M. Yegar, *Islam and Islamic Institutions in British Malaya*, and A. A. Milner, "The Impact of the Turkish Revolution in Malaya."

24. Quoted in Yegar, *Islam and Islamic Institutions*, 110.

25. Ibid., and Milner, "Impact of Turkish Revolution."

26. Milner, "Impact of Turkish Revolution," 118–20.

27. Ibid., 120.

28. "Panislamisme," Overzicht van de Qestie der Centraal Sarekat-Islam in het Jaar 1921 (government report, Dutch East Indies, 1922), 3.

29. See F. R. von der Mehden, *Religion and Nationalism in Southeast Asia.*

30. Quoted in R. McVey, *The Rise of Indonesian Communism*, 161.

31. See ibid.; von der Mehden, *Religion and Nationalism*, 159–61; and B. Herring, "The Sarekat Islam: A Historical Perspective."

32. von der Mehden, *Religion and Nationalism*, 160.

33. Quoted in M. Kramer, *Islam Assembled*, 109.

34. H. Benda, *The Crescent and the Rising Sun*, 221, n. 38.

35. Ibid., 95.

36. See, e.g., J. Peacock, *Muslim Puritans*; F. Abdullah, *Radical Malay Politics*; T. Abdullah, *Schools of Politics: The Kaum Muda Movement in West Sumatra*; H. Federspiel, *Persatuan Islam*; D. Noer, *The Modernist Muslim Movement in Indonesia, 1900–1942*; and Hooker, *Islam in South-East Asia.*

37. A review of the biographies of prominent ulama of the period gives ample evidence of this relationship, with a sizable percentage receiving at least

part of their religious training in the Middle East. See, e.g., K. Steenbrink, *Beberapa Aspek Tentang Islam di Indonesia Abad K-19*. For an interesting study of an individual scholar, see M. Nakamura, "Haji Muzakhir and the Maturing of Indonesian Islam."

38. Roff, "South-East Asian Islam in the Nineteenth Century," 177.

39. There were other issues as well, such as debates over the Ahmadiyya movement and its relation to Islam. See S. bin Ibrahim and J. Syariah, "The Intellectual Conflict between Ahmadiyya and Its Opponents in Pre-War Malaya."

40. See van Bruinessan, "Bukankah" and M. N. bin Ngah, "Some Writing of the Traditional Malay Muslim Scholars Found in Malaysia."

41. See F. Abdullah, *Radical Malay Politics*, 30–31.

42. See M. Rickfels, *A History of Modern Indonesia*, 161–62.

43. Peacock, *Purifying the Faith*.

44. See Alfian, *Muhammadiyah*.

45. World Bank, *World Development Report 1990* (New York: Oxford University Press, 1990), 234.

CHAPTER 2

1. *World Muslim League Magazine* 3 (1966): 64.

2. Ibid. 2 (1964): 64.

3. *Islamic Herald* 5 (1981).

4. O. H. Lee, *Indonesia Facing the 1980s*, 207.

5. *New Straits Times*, April 8, 1978.

6. Ibid., February 1, 1979. See also articles in the *Islamic Herald*, PERKIM's bimonthly magazine, and T. A. Rahman, "PERKIM's Vital Role in Promoting Islam," *Contemporary Issues in Malaysian Politics*.

7. *Al Nahdah* 2, no. 3 (July-September 1982).

8. *New Straits Times*, November 16, 1978.

9. This material is largely from Z. Dhoffier, "The Economic Effect on Indonesia of the Hajj."

10. From 1985 to 1990 the number of pilgrims from Malaysia ranged from a low of 24,415 in 1985 to 36,658 in 1990. *New Straits Times*, June 12, 1990.

11. *Al Nahdah* 8, no. 1 (1988): 63.

12. Dhoffier, "Economic Effect," 58–59. The government also sought to keep numbers down in order to be able to provide a subsidy to pilgrims.

13. Ibid., 60.

14. Ibid., 67.

15. Ibid., 68.

16. *Straits Times*, March 5, 1974.

17. *Economic Review of the Arab World* 3 (August 1969): 47; (September 1969): 15, 16, 69.

18. At that time, the ASEAN states were importing US$2.6 billion from the Middle East and exporting US$367 million. *New Straits Times*, February 19, 1976.

19. United Nations, *Economic Survey of Asia and the Far East 1949* (Lake Success, N.Y.: United Nations Press, 1950), 201.

20. World Bank, *World Development Report 1990* (New York: Oxford University Press, 1990), 178–79, 204–5.

21. E.g., the Saudi Arabian Chamber of Trade expressed its interest in expanding trade with Indonesia after the visit of an Indonesian trade mission in 1974. See *Indonesia Perspectives* (August 1974).

22. See *Iktisadi* for those years.

23. Ibid. 2, no. 12 (July 1981): 3.

24. Ibid. 4, no. 11 (June 1983): 3.

25. Ibid. 4, no. 8 (March 1983): 3.

26. *New Straits Times*, February 17, 1976.

27. C. Wadhva and M. Asher, *ASEAN–South Asia Economic Relations*, 35, 36, 69ff.

28. A country like Singapore exported more industrial products including electronics and plastics.

29. Figures from *Economic Review of the Arab World* (March 1985), June 1990.

30. L. Demery, "Asian Labor Migration: An Empirical Assessment," 27.

31. This does not even take into account a large number of workers going from other East Asian states, particularly South Korea and the People's Republic of China.

32. *Asiaweek*, January 7, 1983.

33. *Straits Times*, February 23, 1983.

34. Ibid., April 7, 1983.

35. C. Stahl, "Southeast Asian Labor in the Middle East," 87.

36. *Christian Science Monitor*, April 17, 1991.

37. *ASEAN Forecast* 5, no. 1 (January 1985).

38. Ibid.

39. Ibid., August 29, 1990.

40. *Far Eastern Economic Review*, August 9, 1990.

41. Another report put Indonesian workers in the UAE (where twenty-eight were soldiers), Jordan, Saudi Arabia, Iraq (up to 1980), Kuwait, and Iran. See *Iktisadi* 4, no. 8 (March 1983): 5.

42. Ibid.

43. Ibid. 4, no. 2 (September 1982): 7.

44. *Asiaweek*, January 7, 1983.

45. *New Straits Times*, June 28, 1979.

46. Ibid., March 30, 1982.

47. "Islamic Development Bank Funds," *Iktisadi* 4, no. 10 (May 1983): 16.

48. *Economic Review of the Arab World* (October 1983).

49. *Economist*, December 10, 1977, 49.

50. Arab Planning Institute, Kuwait Economic Society, seminar on Investment of Arab Oil Producing Countries, mimeo, 1974.

51. Ibid., 155–56.

52. K. Dickie and T. Layman, *Foreign Investment/Government Policy in the Third World*, 128.

53. *Malaysian Business*, December 1, 1987, 49–52.

54. Ibid., 51.

55. *Iktisadi* 2, no. 12 (July 1981): 5.

56. Ibid. 4, no. 8 (1983): 4.

57. *Straits Times*, August 18, September 2, 1977.

58. Ibid., December 13, 1980.

59. *Middle East Economic Digest*, September 14, 1979.

60. K. Dipoyudo, "Indonesia's Foreign Policy towards the Middle East and Africa," 482.

61. *Malaysian Business*, December 1, 1987, 51.

62. Arab Planning Institute, seminar on Investment of Arab Oil Producing Countries.

CHAPTER 3

1. For details, see von der Mehden, "The Political and Social Challenges of the Islamic Revival in Malaysia and Indonesia," and S. Barraclough, "Managing the Challenges of Islamic Revival in Malaysia."

2. Sukarno, "The Birth of Pantja Sila," 18.

3. More recently, a breakaway element of UMNO, Semengat '46, provided another Muslim opponent.

4. Foreign Service Institute, *Diplomatic Agenda of the Philippine Presidents 1946–1985* (Manila, 1985), 80.

5. L. Panganandaman, "Relations with the Countries," 33.

6. K. Dipoyudo, "Indonesia's Foreign Policy," 475.

7. M. Leifer, "The Islamic Factor in Indonesia's Foreign Policy: A Case of Functional Ambiguity," 150.

8. Ibid.

9. F. Weinstein, *Indonesian Foreign Policy and the Dilemma of Dependence*, 128–29; G. Hein, "Soeharto's Foreign Policy."

10. Weinstein, *Indonesian Foreign Policy*, 238.

11. V. Morais, ed., *Strategy for Action*, 346–57.

12. *Foreign Affairs Malaysia* 10, no. 2 (June 1977): 45–46.

13. *New Straits Times*, November 4, 1977.

14. *Straits Times*, May 5, 1985.

15. E.g., see the speech of the Malaysian foreign minister, *Foreign Affairs Malaysia* (1979): 343.

16. "Towards Islamic Solidarity," speech in Saudi Arabia, January 27, 1981, in M. Pathamanathan and D. Lazarus, eds., *The Winds of Change: The Mahathir Impact on Malaysia's Foreign Policy*, 61.

17. *New Straits Times*, August 17, 1987. During that month, there was considerable discussion of Zionist efforts to topple the Malaysian government.

18. *Straits Times*, September 18, 1981.

19. For example, see *Al-Nahdah* 2, no. 4 (December 1982), and *New Straits Times*, July 15, 1982.

20. Dipoyudo, *Trends in Indonesia*.

21. Leifer, "The Islamic Factor," 156.

22. *Iktisadi* 5 (December 10, 1983): 15.

23. Weinstein, *Indonesian Foreign Policy*, 125.

24. *Straits Times*, November 23, 1973.

25. Ibid., April 18, 1979.

26. *New Straits Times*, July 27, 1984.

27. G. Hein, "Soeharto's Foreign Policy," 237.

28. Weinstein, *Indonesian Foreign Policy*, 129.

29. *Al-Nahdah* 4, no. 2 (1984).

30. *Foreign Affairs Malaysia* 14, no. 1 (March 1981): 6.

31. C. Penders, ed., *Milestones on My Journey*, 366–71.

32. See Hein, "Soeharto's Foreign Policy," 231–32.

33. Ibid.

34. *Straits Times Weekly*, January 26, 1991.

35. *Far Eastern Economic Review*, January 24, 1991.

36. For example, the ten Muslim members of the Singapore Parliament warned that Muslims should not be misled by Saddam's efforts to link Kuwait and Palestine. *Straits Times Weekly*, January 26, 1991.

37. See ibid.; *Far Eastern Economic Review*, January 24, 1991; *Christian Science Monitor*, January 31, 1991.

38. *World Muslim League Magazine* 2, no. 8 (July 1965): 63.

39. See Yegar, *The Muslims of Burma*, 99–101.

40. *Al-Nahdah* 8, no. 1 (1988): 57.

41. There is considerable literature on this issue. See, e.g., Kraus, "Islam in Thailand"; A. Forbes, "The Muslims of Thailand"; P. Surin, "Islam and Malay Nationalism: A Case Study of the Malay Muslims of Southern Thailand"; and G. Gunn, "Radical Islam in Southeast Asia."

42. Gunn, "Radical Islam," 37.

43. *Bangkok Post*, April 20, 1985.

44. W. K. C. Man, *Muslim Separatism: The Moros of Southern Philippines and the Malays of Southern Thailand*, 104–10.

45. Like the Thai case, there has been considerable literature on this issue. See L. Noble, "The Moro National Liberation Front in the Philippines," and Noble, "Muslim Separatism in the Philippines, 1972–1981: The Making of a Stalemate"; T. George, *Revolt in Mindanao*; and P. Gowing, *Mosque and Moro: The Study of Muslims in the Philippines*.

46. *New York Times*, June 27, 1991.

47. See J. Piscatori, *International Relations of the Asian Muslim States*, 9–11.

48. George, *Revolt in Mindanao*, 243.

49. *Far Eastern Economic Review*, January 6, February 10, March 3, 1983. In 1980, Saudi Arabia did cut off oil due to the mistreatment of Muslims but, after a visit by Imelda Marcos to Riyadh, reversed the policy.

50. *New York Times*, June 24, 1974. Statement by Foreign Minister Abdel Aty al-Abeidi.

51. H. Mintaredja, *Islam and Politics and State in Indonesia*, 72.

52. For a description of various organizations see M. Kamlin, "The Islamic Conference System: Its Origins, Purposes and Prospects"; C. N. A. Khan, *Commonwealth of Muslim States*; J. Landau, *The Politics of Pan-Islam*; *Journal World Muslim League*; and *Main Documents of the Africa-Asia Islamic Conference, Bandung, 6–14 March, 1965* (Jakarta: Government Printing Office, 1965).

53. Piscatori, *International Relations*, 26.

54. See *Al-Nahdah* 7, no. 1 (1987): 44–45.

55. J. Reinhardt, *Foreign Policy and National Integration: The Case of Indonesia*, 115.

56. Quoted in Hein, "Soeharto's Foreign Policy," 141.

57. Ibid., 242–43.

58. *Iktisadi* 2, no. 2 (September 1980): 3–4.

59. A. R. Perwiranegara, *Development of Indonesian Moslems*, 39.

60. A. Ahmad, *Tengku Abdul Rahman and Malaysia's Foreign Policy, 1963–1970*, 112–13.

CHAPTER 4

1. *Foreign Affairs Malaysia* 12, no. 4 (1979), 463.

2. S. Siddique, "Contemporary Islamic Developments in ASEAN," 90.

3. Malaysia had an embassy in Tehran, but Iran did not have a counterpart in Kuala Lumpur until after the fall of the shah.

4. See *Ekspor Indonesia 1982* (Jakarta: Department of Perdaganaan, 1983); "Five Years of Indonesian Efforts in the Middle East," *Iktisadi* 4, no. 8 (March

1983): 5; and *New Straits Times*, September 29, 30, October 1, 16, 1980. The number of Indonesian workers decreased from 836 in 1977–78 to 0 in the early 1980s.

5. See tables 5–7 in chapter 2.

6. Thailand, *Statistical Yearbook of Thailand 1985* (Bangkok: National Statistical Office), 328.

7. *Straits Times*, July 7, 1979; *Star* (Penang), July 19, 1979.

8. *Star*, October 7, 1982.

9. *New Straits Times*, December 12, 1984.

10. *Straits Times*, January 14, 1984.

11. Barraclough, "Managing the Challenges," 961.

12. TAPOL (Indonesian Human Rights Campaign), *Indonesia: Muslims on Trial*, 81ff.

13. A detailed account of this case was given in *Indonesia Reports—Human Rights Supplement* 18 (October 1986): 5–7, *Indonesia Reports* 13 (November 1985): 36, and 16 (June 1986): 45. Amnesty International has come to the defense of the accused, stating that no violence was intended. For Indonesian human rights concerns, see TAPOL, *Indonesia: Muslims on Trial*.

14. By far the best analysis of the impact of the Iranian Revolution on the Philippines has been C. Majul, "The Iranian Revolution and the Muslims in the Philippines." The bulk of the information in this section is from Majul's piece.

15. *New Straits Times*, August 14, October 3, 1981.

16. Ibid., June 10, 1982. There were also reports of bomb injuries.

17. Majul, "The Iranian Revolution," 271–77.

18. Quoted in ibid., 264.

19. Quoted in ibid., 276.

20. *Far Eastern Economic Review*, August 9, 1990.

21. *New Straits Times*, June 20, 1990.

22. *Straits Times*, July 2, 1990.

23. *Al-Nahdah* 5, no. 3 (1985): 50.

24. *Star*, October 23, 1985.

25. *Berita Harian* (Kuala Lumpur), October 1, 1987.

26. See Barraclough, "Managing the Challenges," and von der Mehden, "Political and Social Challenge."

27. See B. Baried, "L'Islam dans L'Archipel: Le Shi'isme en Indonesie."

28. M. N. Tamara, *Indonesia in the Wake of Islam, 1965–1985*, 6.

29. See M. A. Rais, "International Islamic Movements and Their Influence upon the Islamic Movement in Indonesia," 37–38.

30. E.g., from March 1979 through early 1980, each monthly issue of the Malaysian Muslim journal *Dakwah* included a story on events in Iran, usually containing a picture of Khoumeini and once with his picture on the cover.

31. *Utusan Melayu*, April 2, 4, 1979.

32. See, e.g., "Israel Senag Hati," *Dakwah* 48 (November 1980): 8–9.

33. *Watan* (Kuala Lumpur), May 16, 1979.

34. Ibid., March 11, 1979. He also said that there was nothing to fear from events in Iran and that Khoumeini was trying to bring Sunni and Shi'ites together.

35. Noted in M. Chandra, *Islamic Resurgence in Malaysia*, 36. Chandra also commented that the Revolution was a secondary factor in giving impetus to the Islamic revival in Malaysia.

36. *Indonesia Reports* has published a number of these religious talks in recent years.

37. See M. Chandra, *Islamic Resurgence*.

38. For a discussion of contemporary Indonesian perspectives of this struggle, see A. Samson, "Conceptions of Politics, Power, and Ideology in Contemporary Indonesian Islam," 196–226.

39. Tamara, *Indonesia in the Wake of Islam*, 25.

CHAPTER 5

1. S. Sjahrir, *Out of Exile*. These were letters he wrote during political exile in the 1930s.

2. G. Atiyeh, *The Contemporary Middle East, 1948–1973*.

3. *Star*, February 11, 1983.

4. *New Straits Times*, December 11, 1985.

5. From a three-part study of PAS leader Hadi Awang, ibid., June 13, 1990.

6. Beside PAS, student organizations such as ABIM and Persatuan Kebangsaan Pelajar Islam Malaysia (PKPIM) have maintained close ties to Cairo and the Muslim Brothers.

7. See S. bin. Ibrahim, *The Islamic Party of Malaysia: Its Formative Stages and Ideology*, 74–75.

8. Ibid.

9. *Universiti Malaya Kalendar, 1988–1989*.

10. *Kalendar Universiti Kebangsaan, 1981–82, 1986–87*.

11. A. H. Hassan, "The Development of Islamic Education in Kelantan," 202. Also see M. A. Rauf, "Islamic Education," and J. Nagata, *The Reflowering of Malaysian Islam*.

12. Nagata, *Reflowering*, 31.

13. *Bibliografi Buku-Buku Dalam Bahasa Malaysia 1971–1975* (Kuala Lumpur: Perpustakaan Negara Malaysia, 1982). This was not because of formal bans by the government. A list of books banned at the University of Malaya in 1976 finds no mention of any of the Middle Eastern "revivalists." *Senarai Buku-Buku Terhad Dan Buku-Buku Di Haramakan* (Penang: di Perpustakaan, 1976).

14. See H. Benda, *Crescent and the Rising Sun*, 126–27, 242–43.

15. It is interesting to read Muhammed Kamel Hassan's study of Indonesian Muslim intellectuals written in 1975. In a good review of divisions among the Indonesian intellectual elite there is little mention of postwar Middle Eastern Islamic writers but considerable emphasis on the impact of prewar modernists. See M. K. Hassan, *Muslim Intellectual Responses to "New Order" Modernization in Indonesia*.

16. Tamara, *Indonesia in the Wake of Islam*, 24.

17. Ibid., 6. Tamara observed that a publishing house in Bandung established in 1982 had published more than 100 books on Islam in the three years following its opening.

18. *Diskusi Buku Agama* (Jakarta: Tempo, 1987).

19. *Buku Islam Sejak 1945* (Jakarta: Haji Masagung, 1987).

20. S. Jones, "Arab Instruction and Literacy in Javanese Muslim Schools"; M. Nakamura, "The Radical Traditionalism of the Nahdatul Ulama in Indonesia"; and K. A. Steenbrink, "Pesantren, Madrasah, Sekolah." This is not to argue that Arabic is not of great importance in Indonesian religious writing. See H. Federspiel, "The Political and Social Language of Indonesian Muslims: The Case of Al-Muslimun," 56–57, and J. Bluhm, "A Preliminary Statement on the Dialogue Established Between the Reform Magazine *Al-Manar* and the Malayo-Indonesian World." Religious schools still have a significant percentage of their books in Arabic. In 1980–81 it was noted that the fourteen Islamic universities of Indonesia had 172,367 books in Indonesian, 96,706 in Arabic, 33,085 in English, and 1,039 in other languages. See M. Abaza, "Cultural Exchange and Muslim Education: Indonesian Students in Cairo," 95.

21. D. Bakkar, "The Struggle for the Future: Some Significant Aspects of Contemporary Islam in Indonesia," 129.

22. K. Ahmad and Z. I. Ansari, *Islamic Perspectives*.

23. *Kurikulum dan Silabus Perdidikan Agama Islam Pada Pergruan Tinggi Ummum* (Jakarta: Department of Religion, 1979).

24. Nurcholesh Madjid, "The Progress of Islam and the Reformation Process," 65.

25. Quoted in *Indonesia Reports—Culture & Society Supplement* 25 (August 1988): 2.

26. Ibid., 3.

27. Tamara, *Indonesia in the Wake of Islam*, 25.

28. For an example of this, see *Prisma* 35 (March 1985), an issue dedicated to Islam in Indonesia.

29. Steenbrink, "Pesantren," 173.

30. A. Ahmad, ed., *Dakwah Islam dan Perubahan Sosial*.

31. Interviews, Jakarta, June 1990. Many stated that it still remained important in places such as south Sulawesi.

32. The most complete analysis of the impact of Al-Azhar on Indonesian Islam is Abaza's "Cultural Exchange." Much of the material in this section has been developed from this dissertation.

33. Ibid., 131–33.

34. *Indonesia Reports* 24 (November 1987): 30.

35. See Abaza, "Cultural Exchange," 177ff.

36. Ibid.

37. Still, Noer states that the majority of the ministers of religious affairs have been educated in the Middle East. See D. Noer, *Administration of Islam in Indonesia*, 15–16.

38. Abaza, "Cultural Exchange," 178.

39. Ibid., 130.

40. See, e.g., S. Taouti, "The Forgotten Muslims of Kampuchea and Viet Nam."

41. E.g., the Burmese press found it important enough to note that 150 people left for the pilgrimage on June 4, 1991. *Burma Press Summary* 5, no. 6 (June 1991): 17.

42. M. K. Hassan, "Some Dimensions of Islamic Education in Southeast Asia," 46–48.

43. Man, *Muslim Separatism*, 58.

44. N. Madale, "The Resurgence of Islam and Nationalism in the Philippines," 289–90.

45. Majul, "The Iranian Revolution," 258.

46. Noted in Madale, "The Resurgence of Islam," 286.

47. Man, *Muslim Separatism*, 161–62.

Selected Bibliography

BOOKS AND ARTICLES

Abaza, M. "Cultural Exchange and Muslim Education: Indonesian Students in Cairo." Ph.D. diss., Bielefeld, 1990.

Abdullah, F. *Radical Malay Politics*. Petaling Jaya: Pelanduk, 1985.

Abdullah, T. *Schools of Politics: The Kaum Muda Movement in West Sumatra*. Ithaca: Cornell Modern Indonesia Project, 1971.

Ahmad, A. *Tengku Abdul Rahman and Malaysia's Foreign Policy, 1963–1970*. Kuala Lumpur: Berita, 1985.

———, ed. *Dakwah Islam dan Perubahan Sosial*. Yogyakarta: Prima Dutu, 1983.

Ahmad, K., and Z. I. Ansari. *Islamic Perspectives*. London: Islamic Foundation, 1979.

Alfian. *Muhammadiyah*. Yogyakarta: Gadjah Mada Press, 1989.

Ali, M. "Pakistan-Indonesia: Ties of Amity." *Pakistan Horizon* 34 (1981): 93–108.

Ann, L., ed. *Economic Relations between West Asia and Southeast Asia*. Singapore: Institute of Southeast Asian Studies, 1978.

Arnold, F., and N. Shah, eds. *Asian Labor Migration*. Boulder: Westview, 1986.

Atiyeh, G. *The Contemporary Middle East, 1948–1973*. Boston: G.K. Hall, 1975.

Bakkar, D. "The Struggle for the Future: Some Significant Aspects of Contemporary Islam in Indonesia." *Muslim World* 62 (April 1972): 126–36.

Bareid, B. "L'Islam dans L'Archipel: Le Shi'isme en Indonesie." *Archipel* 15 (1978): 65–84.

Barraclough, S. "Managing the Challenges of Islamic Revival in Malaysia." *Asian Survey* 23 (August 1983): 958–75.

Benda, H. *The Crescent and the Rising Sun*. The Hague: Van Hoeve, 1958.

Bluhm, J. "A Preliminary Statement on the Dialogue Established between the Reform Magazine *Al-Manar* and the Malayo-Indonesian World." *Indonesian Circle* 32 (November 1983): 35–73.

Boland, B. *The Struggle of Islam in Modern Indonesia*. The Hague: Nijhoff, 1971.

Boyce, P. *Malaysia and Singapore in International Diplomacy*. Sydney: Sydney University Press, 1968.

Chandra, M. *Islamic Resurgence in Malaya*. Petaling Jaya: Penerbit Fajar Bakti, 1987.

Chauduri, K. "Indonesia in the Early Seaborne Trade of the Indian Ocean." *Indonesia Circle* 33 (March 1984): 3–13.

Dawisha, A., ed. *Islam and Foreign Policy*. Cambridge: Cambridge University Press, 1983.

de Graaf, H. and T. Pigeaud. *De Eerste Moslimisme Vorstendommen op Java*. The Hague: Nijhoff, 1976.

Demery, L. "Asian Labor Migration: An Empirical Assessment." In *Asian Labor Migration*, edited by F. Arnold and N. Shah, 17–46. Boulder: Westview, 1986.

Dhoffier, Z. "The Economic Effect on Indonesia of the Hajj." *Prisma* 36 (June 1985): 56–68.

Dickie, K., and T. Layman. *Foreign Investment/Government Policy in the Third World*. New York: St. Martin's Press, 1988.

Dipoyudo, K. "Indonesia's Foreign Policy towards the Middle East and Africa." *Indonesia Quarterly* 13, no. 4 (October 1985): 475–85.

———. *Trends in Indonesia*. Jakarta: CSIS, 1981.

Engineer, A., ed. *Islam in South and Southeast Asia*. Delhi: Ajanta, 1983.

Esposito, J., ed. *The Iranian Revolution: The Global Impact*. Miami: Florida International University Press, 1990.

Evangelista, O. "Some Aspects of the History of Islam in Southeast Asia." In *Understanding Islam and Muslims in the Philippines*, edited by P. Gowing, 16–25. Quezon City: New Day, 1988.

Federspiel, H. *Persatuan Islam*. Ithaca: Cornell Monograph Series, 1970.

———. "The Political and Social Language of Indonesian Muslims: The Case of Al-Muslimun." *Indonesia* 31 (October 1984): 55–73.

Forbes, A., ed. "The Muslims of Thailand." *South East Asian Review* 14 (January–December 1989): 1–112.

George, T. *Revolt in Mindanao*. Kuala Lumpur: Oxford University Press, 1980.

Gowing, P. *Mosque and Moro: The Study of Muslims in the Philippines*. Manila: Philippine Federation of Christian Churches, 1964.

———, ed. *Understanding Islam and Muslims in the Philippines*. Quezon City: New Day, 1988.

Gunn, G. "Radical Islam in Southeast Asia." *Journal of Contemporary Asia* 16 (1986): 30–54.

Hassan, A. H. "The Development of Islamic Education in Kelantan." In *Tamadin di Malaysia*, edited by K. K. Lim et al. Kuala Lumpur: Persatuan Sejarah Malaysia, 1980.

Hassan, M. K. *Muslim Intellectual Responses to "New Order" Modernization in Indonesia*. Kuala Lumpur: Dewan Bahasa Pustaka, 1980.

———. "Some Dimensions of Islamic Education in Southeast Asia." In *Islam and Society in Southeast Asia*, edited by T. Abdullah and S. Siddique, 40–79. Singapore: Institute of Southeast Asian Studies, 1986.

Hefner, R. "Islamizing Java? Religion and Politics in Rural East Java." *Journal of Asian Studies* 46, no. 3 (August 1987): 533–54.

Hein, G. "Soeharto's Foreign Policy: Second Generation Nationalism in Indonesia." Ph.D. diss., University of California, Berkeley, 1986.

Herring, B. "The Sarekat Islam: A Historical Perspective." *Studies on Islam*, Occasional Paper No. 22. Towneville, Australia: James Cook University, 1987.

Hill, H. *Foreign Investment and Indigenization in Indonesia*. Singapore: Oxford University Press, 1988.

Hooker, M. B., ed. *Islam in South-East Asia*. Leiden: Brill, 1983.

Hunter, S. *The Politics of Islamic Revivalism*. Bloomington: Indiana University Press, 1988.

Ibrahim, A., and S. Siddique, eds. *Readings on Islam in Southeast Asia*. Singapore: Institute of Southeast Asian Studies, 1985.

Ibrahim, S. bin *The Islamic Party of Malaysia: Its Formative Stages and Ideology*. Pasir Puteh, Kelantan: Nuawi bin Ismail, 1981.

Ibrahim, S. bin, and J. Syariah. "The Intellectual Conflict between Ahmadiyya and Its Opponents in Pre-War Malaya." *Jebat* 15 (1987): 3–18.

Johns, A. H. "Islam in Southeast Asia." *Indonesia* 19 (1975): 33–55.

Jones, S. "Arab Instruction and Literacy in Javanese Muslim Schools." *Prisma* 21 (June 1981): 71–80.

Joo-Jack, L. "West and Southeast Asia: Sharing Common Concerns." In *Economic Relations between West Asia and Southeast Asia*, edited by L. S. Ann. Singapore: Institute of Southeast Asian Studies, 1978.

Kamarun, K. "Sejarah Haji di Malaysia." *Dakwah* (August 1986): 8–12.

Kamlin, M. "The Islamic Conference System: Its Origins, Purposes and Prospects." *Kandungan* 2 (1974–75): 44–62.

Khan, C. N. A. *Commonwealth of Muslim States*. Karachi: Ferozoomo, 1972.

Kramer, M. *Islam Assembled*. New York: Columbia University Press, 1986.

Kraus, W. "Islam in Thailand." *Journal of the Institute of Muslim Minority Affairs* (July 1984): 410–24.

Kumar, A. *A Diary of a Javanese Muslim*. Canberra: Faculty of Asian Studies No. 7. Australian National University, 1985.

Landau, J. *The Politics of Pan-Islam*. London: Clarendon Press, 1990.

Lee, O. H. *Indonesia Facing the 1980s*. Hull: Europress, 1979.

Leifer, M. "The Islamic Factor in Indonesia's Foreign Policy: A Case of

Functional Ambiguity." In *Islam and Foreign Policy,* edited by A. Dawisha, 144–59. Cambridge: Cambridge University Press, 1983.

Lim, K. K., et al. *Tamadun Di Malaysia.* Kuala Lumpur: Persatuan Sejarah Malaysia, 1980.

McVey, R. *The Rise of Indonesian Communism.* Ithaca: Cornell University Press, 1965.

Madale, N. "The Resurgence of Islam and Nationalism in the Philippines." In *Islam and Society in Southeast Asia,* edited by T. Abdullah and S. Siddique. Singapore: Institute of Southeast Asian Studies, 1986.

Madjid, N. "The Progress of Islam and the Reformation Process." *Mizan* 1, no. 11 (1985): 61–66.

Majul, C. "The Iranian Revolution and the Muslims in the Philippines." In *The Iranian Revolution: The Global Impact,* edited by J. Esposito, 258–80. Miami: Florida International University Press, 1990.

Malaysia. *Bibliografi Buku-Buku Dalam Bahasa Malaysia, 1971–1975.* Kuala Lumpur: Perpustakaan Negara Malaysia, 1982.

———. *Senarai Buku-Buku Terhad Dan Buku-Buku di Haramakan.* Penang: Di Perpustakaan, 1976.

Man, W. K. C. *Muslim Separatism: The Moros of Southern Philippines and the Malays of Southern Thailand.* Singapore: Oxford University Press, 1990.

Milner, A. A. "The Impact of the Turkish Revolution in Malaya." *Archipel* 31 (1986): 117–30.

Mintaredja, H. *Islam and Politics and State in Indonesia.* Siliwangi: N.p., 1974.

Morais, V., ed. *Strategy for Action.* Kuala Lumpur: Malaysian Centre for Development Studies, 1969.

Mursyidi, H. *Sumuran Harahap Lintasan Sejarah Perjalanan Jemaah Haji Indonesia.* Jakarta: Melton Putra, 1984.

Nagata, J. *The Reflowering of Malaysian Islam.* Vancouver: University of British Columbia Press, 1984.

Nakamura, M. "The Crescent Arises over the Banyan Tree." Ph.D. diss., Cornell University, 1976.

———. "Haji Muzakhir and the Maturing of Indonesian Islam." *Mizan* 1, no. 3 (1984): 87–97.

———. "The Radical Traditionalism of the Nahdatul Ulama in Indonesia." Mimeo. Canberra: Australian National University, 1980.

Natsir, M. "Masa depan Hubungan Indonesia." *Budaya Java* 9 (March 1976): 166–81.

Ngah, M. N. bin. "Some Writing of the Traditional Malay Muslim Scholars Found in Malaysia." In *Tamadun di Malaysia,* edited by K. K. Lim et al. Kuala Lumpur: Persatuan Sejarah Malaysia, 1980.

Noble, L. "The Moro National Liberation Front in the Philippines." *Pacific Affairs* 49, no. 3 (Fall 1976): 405–24.

———. "Muslim Separatism in the Philippines, 1972–1981: The Making of a Stalemate." *Asian Survey* 31 (December 1981): 1097–1114.

Noer, D. *Administration of Islam in Indonesia*. Ithaca: Cornell Modern Indonesia Project, 1978.

———. *The Modernist Muslim Movement in Indonesia, 1900–1942*. London: Oxford University Press, 1973.

Panganandaman, L. "Relations with the Countries." *Kasayan* 5 (1980): 32–36.

Pathamanathan, M., and D. Lazarus, eds. *The Winds of Change: The Mahathir Impact on Malaysia's Foreign Policy*. Kuala Lumpur: Eastview Productions, 1984.

Peacock, J. *Muslim Puritans*. Berkeley: University of California Press, 1978.

———. *Purifying the Faith*. Menlo Park, Calif.: Benjamin/Cummings, 1978.

Penders, C., ed. *Milestones on My Journey: Memoirs of Ali Sastroamidjojo*. St. Lucia: University of Queensland Press, 1979.

Perwiranegara, A. R. *Development of Indonesian Moslems*. Jakarta: Government of Indonesia, 1979.

Philippines. *Diplomatic Agenda of Philippine Presidents, 1946–1985*. Manila: Foreign Service Institute, 1985.

Piscatori, J. *International Relations of the Asian Muslim States*. Lanham, Md.: University Press of America, 1986.

Pitsuan, S. "Islam and Malay Nationalism: A Case Study of the Malay Muslims of Southern Thailand." Ph.D. diss., Harvard University, 1980.

Rahman, T. A. "PERKIM's Vital Role in Promoting Islam." In *Contemporary Issues in Malaysian Politics*, 291–300. Peladuk, 1984.

Rais, M. A. "International Islamic Movements and Their Influence upon the Islamic Movement in Indonesia." *Prisma* 35 (March 1985): 27–48.

Rauf, M. A. "Islamic Education." *Intisari* 11, no. 1: 14–31.

Reid, A. *The Contest for North Sumatra*. Kuala Lumpur: Oxford University Press, 1969.

———. "Nineteenth-Century Pan-Islam in Indonesia and Malaysia." *Journal of Asian Studies* 26 (February 1967): 267–83.

———. "Sixteenth-Century Turkish Influence in Western Indonesia." *Journal of Southeast Asian History* 10, no. 3 (December 1969): 395–414.

———. *Southeast Asia in the Age of Commerce*. Vol. 1. New Haven: Yale University Press, 1988.

Reinhardt, J. *Foreign Policy and National Integration: The Case of Indonesia*. New Haven: Yale University Southeast Asia Monograph Series, No. 17, 1971.

Rickfels, M. *A History of Modern Indonesia*. Bloomington: Indiana University Press, 1981.

Roff, W. "Indonesian and Malay Students in Cairo in the 1920s." *Indonesia* 9 (April 1970): 73–87.

———. "South-East Asian Islam in the Nineteenth Century." In *The*

Cambridge History of Islam, edited by P. Holt et al., vol. 2, 155–81. Cambridge: Cambridge University Press, 1970.

Rosenthal, E. *Islam and the Modern National State*. Cambridge: Cambridge University Press, 1965.

Samson, A. "Conceptions of Politics, Power, and Ideology in Contemporary Indonesian Islam." In *Political Power and Communications in Indonesia*, edited by K. Jackson and L. Pye, 196–226. Berkeley: University of California Press, 1978.

Siddique, S. "Contemporary Islamic Developments in ASEAN." In *Southeast Asian Affairs 1980*. Singapore: Institute of Southeast Asian Studies, 1980, 78–90.

Sjahrir, S. *Out of Exile*. New York: John Day, 1949.

Steenbrink, K. A. *Beberapa Aspek Tentang Islam di Indonesia Abad K-19*. Jakarta: Butan Bintang, 1984.

———. "Pesantren, Madrasah, Sekolah." Ph.D. diss., Katholieke Universiteit (Nijmagan), 1974.

Sukarno. *Toward Freedom and the Dignity of Man*. Jakarta: Department of Foreign Affairs, 1961.

Suminto, H. A. *Politik Islam Hindia Belanda*. Jakarta: LP3ES, 1985.

———. "Relations between the Ottoman Empire and the Muslim Kingdoms of the Malay-Indonesian Archipelago." *Der Islam* 57 (1980): 301–10.

Surin, P. "Islam and Malay Nationalism: A Case Study of the Malay Muslims of Southern Thailand." Ph.D. diss., Harvard University, 1980.

Tamara, M. N. *Indonesia in the Wake of Islam, 1965–1985*. Kuala Lumpur: Institute of Strategic Studies Malaysia, 1986.

Taouti, S. "The Forgotten Muslims of Kampuchea and Viet Nam." *Journal of the Institute of Muslim Minority Affairs* 1–2 (1982): 3–13.

TAPOL. *Indonesia: Muslims on Trial*. Guildford, U.K.: Biddles Ltd., 1987.

Tjandrasasmita, U. "The Arrival and Expansion of Islam in Indonesia in Relation to Southeast Asia." *International Seminar on Islam in Southeast Asia*. Jakarta: Lembaga Penelitian lain Syarit Hidayatullah, 1986.

van Bruinessan, M. "Bukankah Orang Kurdi yan Mengistlainkan Indonesia?" *Pesantren* 4, no. 4 (1987): 45–53.

———. "Tarekat Qadiriyah dan Ilmu Syeikh Qadir Jilani di India, Kurdistan, dan Indonesia." *Ulumul Qur'an* 2, no. 2 (1989): 65–77.

van der Muelen, D. *Don't You Hear the Thunder?* Leiden: Brill, 1981.

von der Mehden, F. R. "The Political and Social Challenge of the Islamic Revival in Malaysia and Indonesia." *Muslim World* 76 (July–October 1986): 219–33.

———. *Religion and Modernization in Southeast Asia*. Syracuse: Syracuse University Press, 1986.

————. *Religion and Nationalism in Southeast Asia*. Madison: University of Wisconsin Press, 1963.

Vredenbregt, J. "The Haddj." *Bijdragen Tot de Land- Taal-en Volkenkunde* 118 (1962): 91–154.

Wadhva, C., and M. Asher. *ASEAN–South Asia Economic Relations*. Singapore: Institute of Southeast Asian Studies, 1985.

Weinstein, F. *Indonesian Foreign Policy and the Dilemma of Dependence*. Ithaca: Cornell University Press, 1976.

Wherry, E., et al., eds. *Islam and Missions*. New York: Revell, 1911.

Williams, M. *Communism, Religion, and Revolt in Bantem*. Athens: Ohio University Southeast Asia Series No. 86, 1990.

Yegar, M. *Islam and Islamic Institutions in British Malaya*. Jerusalem: Magnus Press, 1979.

————. *The Muslims of Burma*. Wiesbaden: Otto Harrassowitz, 1970.

Yusuf, Y. "Muhammadiyah: Reformist Ideals and Social Reality." *Mizan* 1, no. 11 (1985): 49–60.

NEWSPAPERS AND MAGAZINES

Al-Nahdah

Al-Risalah (Malaysia)

Asiaweek

Burma Press Summary

Christian Science Monitor

Dakwah (Indonesia)

Dakwah (Malaysia)

Economic Review of the Arab World

Economist

Far Eastern Economic Review

Foreign Affairs Malaysia

Iktisadi

Indonesia Perspectives

Indonesia Reports

Islamic Herald

Malaysian Business

New Straits Times

New York Times

Risalah (Kuala Lumpur)

Singapore Business

Star (Penang)

Straits Times

Straits Times Weekly

Utusan Melayu

Watan

Index